AND THE NIGHT

SHALL BE NO MORE

AND THE NIGHT
SHALL BE NO MORE

BY

GLENN SANDERFUR

A.R.E. Press • Virginia Beach • Virginia

A.R.E. Press
Sixty-Eighth & Atlantic Avenue
P.O. Box 656
Virginia Beach, VA 23451-0656

Library of Congress Cataloging-in-Publication Data
Sanderfur, Glenn, 1934-
    And the night shall be no more / by Glenn Sanderfur.
        p.   cm.
    ISBN 0-87604-305-8
    1. Parapsychology and medicine—Case studies.   2.
Sanderfur, Glenn.   3. Life change events—Case studies.   4.
Cayce, Edgar, 1877-1945.   Edgar Cayce readings.   I. Title.   II.
Title: And the night shall be no more.
BF1045.M44S26 1993
131—dc20   93-17425
Cover illustration by John Hickey
Cover design by Patti McCambridge

DEDICATION

This book is dedicated in loving memory and appreciation to all my Search for God study group members, both in Kentucky and in Virginia, and especially to Tom Ballard and Lynn Weber.

I also want to note and remember those many friends with paralytic injuries whose condition and recovery never permitted them the opportunities and enjoyment of life with which I have been blessed. I salute each of them. Their courage, perseverance, and example have enriched my life and will always outshine and eclipse their suffering and unfulfilled dreams.

When I lie down, I say,
When shall I arise, and the night be gone?
Job 7:4, KJV

CHAPTER ONE

Somewhere in the distance someone shouted, "Shut up!"

Or had I really heard such a thing? I wasn't sure, and yet I felt that maybe I had heard the order more than once. It seemed as if the curt, shrill voice was that of a female. Who was she? And to whom was she talking? I thought I heard the command again but wasn't sure.

"Shut up! You ain't seen nothing yet. It'll get worse before it gets better." There was no doubting the voice or message this time.

It was some time before I realized she was speaking to me. I also became aware of excruciating pain in my legs and was surprised to discover that I was groaning and crying aloud because of the pain. I had no idea where I was. Everything except the constant pain seemed unreal—sort of dream-like. My consciousness faded in and out.

At one point, I realized a woman was doing something to my wrist, and I asked her where I was. She told me I was in the hospital, but doing fine.

Why was I in a hospital? I could remember nothing that would explain my condition. Why wasn't I at home or at work? What time was it? I asked her.

The nurse told me it was seven something. A little later I found out it was seven in the morning.

I was truly stunned. How could I be here? I couldn't move

1

my body, and the pain in my legs was continuing and seemed unbearable at times. It was a shooting, searing pain, worse than anything I had ever experienced. I also became aware of various tubes and other kinds of restraints entering or tied to my body. Whenever I tried to move, I had a sharp pain in my abdomen. At some point, I discovered there was also pain in my back.

A nurse or someone told me that my parents were here, and I would get to see them before long. How could my parents be present? They lived over a hundred miles away in western Kentucky. I was in Louisville.

Over the next hour or so, events continued to be jumbled in my mind; reality was fleeting. But gradually I became more perceptive, and bit by bit I learned more of my situation.

At one point, a doctor appeared and began talking to me. He introduced himself as Dr. Lolley. He told me I had been shot and had had a close call. The bullet had done a lot of damage, and during the night it had been touch-and-go whether I would survive. He was pleased with events so far but warned me that I was still in an extremely critical condition. He said something about my liver and his operation to repair the damage. He indicated it was an unorthodox operation but that he had done it before with successful results. He also said the bullet hit my spine, but they had not yet assessed the effects of this injury. The first priority was to save my life.

After he left, I had many questions. How had I been shot? I could remember being in my apartment the night before and getting ready to go to bed. I had earlier been to a dinner and get-together with fellow employees from the bank where I worked. I was pleased that at least I had taken a shower the night before; there was no telling when I would get one again in the hospital. I don't know why that was important to me at the moment; there were far more important things for me to be thinking about now.

As I combed my memory, I thought I could remember Tom Ballard, my friend, calling my name. There was a frantic urgency in his voice, and I had run to the front of my apartment, opened the door, and gone into the entry hall between the front door and the stairway leading down to Tom's apartment in the basement. I could also recall something happening, like the sudden impact of running into a solid wall. Was this when I was shot? I couldn't remember seeing anyone, nor was I sure I could recall any details after that. I thought maybe I could remember Tom telling me to hold on and that he had called for help. There was also some kind of vague recollection of being in a vehicle; it seemed that I was lying on my back and someone was talking, but I couldn't remember what was said. Beyond those fragments of recollection, I could recall nothing about what had happened to me, and I wasn't sure they actually had occurred.

The next few hours were filled with pain and a kaleidoscope of jumbled activity. Every few minutes a new face would appear to do something or perform some kind of check. I had also discovered a new pain. Whenever I took a deep breath, there was a stabbing hurt in my right chest. They were giving me medicine now to reduce the pains, but I still hurt so badly I seriously wondered if I could stand it. I had never had to contend with severe pain, at least for any length of time, and I had doubts about how I would respond. Surely, though, it would be just a matter of time before I would begin to heal, and the worst would be over.

I was also certain the doctor was overstating the seriousness of my condition. Of course, I was hurting, but I was now fully conscious, so I couldn't be in a critical condition. Did critical mean I might die? I couldn't believe I was close to dying; I would feel differently if I were. But how does one feel just before death? I was pondering questions I had never before had to face; I didn't have any previous experience to compare in the circumstances I was now encountering. I began to realize that I was going to have to draw upon every source of energy and reserve within me to get through this ordeal.

The pain was getting worse, and my inability to move or even turn my body was causing emotional agony. I began to have feelings of claustrophobia. I had to get up; I couldn't just lie here as though I were tied down. But no matter what my mind said or felt, I couldn't rise. I was restricted by medical paraphernalia, and I couldn't move the lower part of my body. I had an overwhelming, panicky feeling that I would be stuck in this position forever—or at least longer than I could stand it.

Another nurse came by my bed and told me that my parents would be in soon. I had forgotten. Why weren't they already here? It had been a long time since I was first told they were present. I wondered what my reaction would be when I saw them? I knew they would be concerned about my condition, and Mother would probably be emotional.

It was actually another hour, sometime after eleven o'clock, before they arrived. It was very good to see them. We had always had a warm, loving relationship, although I usually saw them only three or four times a year—at least since I had moved to Louisville nearly ten years ago. At that time, I had left private law practice in Owensboro, Kentucky, to become a corporate bank attorney.

Waiting now for them to come in, I remembered being with them at their home in Hartford just two weeks previously during the Christmas holidays. Once they entered, neither of them was as emotional as I had thought they might be. Mother wasn't crying, nor did she do so during our brief visit.

"Why did you come up?" I asked. I don't remember now their answer. I told them I was doing fine and that they shouldn't have made the trip.

Then I asked them what had happened. They told me there had been a shooting the night before. Suddenly it occurred to me that Tom Ballard must have been killed. Their vagueness about what had happened reinforced my concern. They assured me, however, that Tom was O.K. He also had been injured, but was doing fine. I wasn't able to get many more details out of them; they claimed they really didn't know much themselves. They said that Tom had called them in the middle of the night and told them to come to Louisville immediately, that I had been shot, and that it was very bad. They had been there since five in the morning, but they couldn't get in to see me sooner. They said they were going to stay in town for awhile and would be back to visit later in the day. The nurse then came up and told them they had to leave.

I needed to see Tom Ballard. Maybe I could learn from him what had happened. I became suspicious again that he really had been killed. He and I were good friends, and they probably thought I wouldn't be able to handle that additional complication if he were in fact dead. That was probably why they hadn't told me. Until I actually saw him, I would have doubts whether I was being told the full story.

I began to pray. I prayed for Tom. I prayed for myself. I even prayed for whoever had shot me; maybe he needed my prayers more than anyone else.

Agonizing and painful hours followed, one after another. The procession of regular technician visits was beginning. People were continually taking blood samples, doing something to the IV tube that entered a vein on the top of my right wrist, giving me pills or medication to swallow, requiring me to breathe into a strange apparatus they put in my mouth, and forever pricking my legs and lower abdomen with a pin and asking if I could feel it. I could not. Various doctors came by and asked me to move my legs, my feet, even my toes, but the result was always negative. I couldn't understand why they didn't collaborate; why did each one have to go through the same routine? But something bigger than this annoyance over procedure was beginning to take shape in my mind: I realized that I had no feeling and was paralyzed from the waist down.

The tests and procedures continued. The worst ordeal was the taking of x-rays. With a portable x-ray machine, they could take a picture at my bed, but it was an awful experience. A flat, square plate had to go under my back, and someone had to lift me up to put it under me. The pain was terrible, and the technician always seemed to be some pretty but frail young woman who wasn't strong enough to lift me up with one hand and get the plate under me with the other. But she would try and try and finally take a picture. Thirty minutes later she or someone frailer would be back for another effort because the earlier picture hadn't turned out right. The plate hadn't been under me far enough. Once—and I think only once—a large, strong man arrived to take the x-ray, and it turned out to be an amazingly simple process.

Late in the afternoon, my parents came back for another brief visit. I had learned that I was in the Intensive Care Unit of Louisville General Hospital and that a ten-minute visit was allowed twice a day. I told my father to be sure they let Tom come in for a visit, that I had many questions only he could answer. He said he would see that the hospital staff would let him visit.

Around five in the afternoon, Dr. Lolley and six or eight young doctors came by for an examination. Dr. Lolley explained my condition to what were obviously students or interns, and I learned more about my status from their conversation.

He explained that I had arrived at the hospital at 11:30 the night before. He called me a "GSI"; I learned later that was the abbreviation for gunshot injury. I was unconscious and hadn't been expected to live because of internal bleeding. Immediate surgery revealed that the artery from the heart to the liver was ruptured and bleeding. The surgeon had then performed some kind of special procedure; I couldn't understand his terms. I learned later that it involved tying the damaged artery and letting the body reroute a channel or flow through a vein to the liver; Dr. Lolley was the only doctor in the area who had ever performed such an operation. I also found out that the bullet had hit the lower part of my right lung and even damaged my pancreas. The students asked a number of questions, and a few started the pin-pricking routine over again. Eventually they moved on to the next patient in the Intensive Care Unit.

Every thirty minutes during waking hours and once during normal sleeping time, I was given inhalation therapy. I had to breath for several minutes through a tube which I held in my mouth. Deep breathing was required, and it was very painful in my right lung. The attendant told me the deep breathing and the medication I received intravenously through a machine were intended to prevent me from getting pneumonia. I found out my constant reclining bed posture made me quite susceptible to this infectious disease and that I was in no condition to combat it if I contracted it.

My leg pains were awful; I had never imagined such pain existed. Combining all the pain I had experienced previously in my life wouldn't begin to amount to the pain I had endured since awakening that morning, the 9th of January, 1974. I was thankful the day was over; at least I had handled it better than I normally might have thought possible.

The night also was difficult, but I slept from time to time with the aid of medication. Near midnight, I completed the first twenty-four hours of what I came to term the long night of the soul.

CHAPTER TWO

Morning arrived, and it was welcomed. At least I could look forward to some more visits—from the doctors, if no one else. Actually, it is impossible to be certain whether it is night or day in the Intensive Care Unit; there are no windows. But there is still something different about nights in a hospital; they are long, boring, and depressing.

I wondered when I would get to see someone from the Federal Intermediate Credit Bank, where I worked. How were they getting along without me? I was the president and chief executive officer, but there were many good officers and department heads, and I was sure that everything was under control. Suddenly I remembered that I had been scheduled to fly to Washington today for a meeting. It was funny how things that had formerly seemed important so quickly assumed a different priority.

Later that morning my parents arrived for their brief visit. They relayed calls of encouragement from the mayor of Louisville, who was a neighbor and friend, from my boss in Washington, the governor of the Farm Credit Administration, and from others. Their messages were comforting. Then my parents said they were going to let Tom Ballard come for the rest of the allowed visiting time and that they would see me in the afternoon.

I was greatly relieved to see Tom walk in and know that

he had in fact survived. He had a bandage on his head and said he had received a concussion, but was otherwise O.K. He then filled me in with details that had been so tantalizingly absent thus far:

Before I had arrived home on Tuesday evening, someone knocked on the front door. Tom and I shared the same entry hall and front door. Two young men were at the door and said they wanted to come in. Before Tom could respond, they walked in and told him to show them around the house. He feared they were up to no good and took them to his apartment rather than remain in the area we shared on the first floor. He hoped to be able to stall them for the moment.

I came home about then, and my arrival resulted in a brief respite. They knew the name of the woman who rented my second floor apartment and had Tom look up her number in the phone book. They called her, but she hung up. When they asked Tom for a rope with which to tie him up, he objected and began a scuffle. They each pulled a gun, and he at that point hollered my name for help. One of the men hit Tom over the head with his handgun, and they both ran up the stairs. They probably would have left without further damage at this point, but I had come into the front entry hall in response to Tom's call and was standing between them and the front door. One of them shot me. Then they ran out of the house. Tom had called the police even before coming to check on my condition.

I lived on a courtyard in a restored area of old Victorian homes in Louisville. A passerby on the court saw two men with guns run from my house. The front door was still open and he could see me lying on the floor. He began shouting that a man had been shot, and neighbors and others arrived just ahead of the police. They put me on a stretcher and immediately took me to General Hospital. The police radioed the hospital, and Dr. Lolley was waiting for me in the emergency room when I arrived.

Tom, too, was treated later at the hospital, then he talked to the police. They accused him of shooting me and said I was now dead. They told him he was guilty of murder. Finally they took a written statement of the events from him and let him go.

No sooner had Tom finished giving me all these details when the nurse arrived to tell Tom his time was up. He departed after assuring me that he was taking care of my apartment and my dog, Vickie. I felt much better after his visit. At least I now had an idea of what had happened. I couldn't recall seeing either of my assailants and, until now, had assumed that it had been only one person. Would they come back? I fervently hoped the police would catch them soon.

Later that day, two detectives came by to see me. At first they were polite, but soon their tone took on an accusative, belligerent quality. I told them everything I could remember. They kept asking me if I knew someone by the name of Jarboe, but I had no idea what or whom they were talking about. I later found out that Jarboe was the name of the person passing my house when the attackers exited and who shouted for help. I suppose it is the duty of law enforcement officials to investigate every angle and that Jarboe's presence seemed to them a possibility they shouldn't overlook. Tom told me later that the police threatened to take Jarboe into custody the night of the incident on suspicion of shooting and possibly murder.

The nurse finally told the detectives they had to leave.

The rounds of doctors' and technicians' visits continued throughout the day. It was no easier than the first day. I wondered who had shot me. Was it someone I knew? Apparently not, based on what Tom had said. But why had the two would-be robbers chosen my house? They had known the name of the second-floor tenant, but they could have obtained that from the side-door mailbox. There were still too many unanswered questions. I hoped that the police would pursue every lead and make an early arrest. If not, was there a risk they might come back? As much as I tried not to, I couldn't avoid worrying about the danger to Tom, myself, or my apartment building from these unknown intruders who were now familiar with the location. I tried to put such disturbing thoughts out of my mind and concentrate on the immediate task of getting well—or possibly of just surviving.

The pain hadn't diminished any, and there seemed to be more activity and tasks to perform than the first day. There were hourly blood samples and x-rays, plus new medicines and procedures to try. I continued to be the subject of curiosity for medical professionals and technicians. One doctor flew in from Louisiana just to witness this kind of case in which, it was hoped, a new artery to the liver was being formed. The day dragged on interminably and painfully.

That second night was just as long and as difficult as the first had been.

The next morning I was allowed a visit from Martin Bonar, executive vice president of the Farm Credit Bank where I worked. He assured me that everything was going fine and urged me just to concentrate on getting well. He had a few questions requiring my input on pending matters, but I was pleased that things were going smoothly at work and that we had people like him working for the bank. Martin then told me that the bank and all thirty-nine of the Production Credit Associations that reported to us in the states of Kentucky, Indiana, Ohio, and Tennessee were pausing at nine o'clock each morning for fifteen minutes of silence or prayer in my behalf. I was stunned at such concern and action, and I realized that it involved over 1,200 employees in more than 200 locations.

Martin's visit was a great morale booster. Later, my parents told me I had received many get-well cards in the mail. I would receive the same story for numerous days to come. Such support was invaluable.

Dr. Lolley came by later in the day for an update on my condition. He said he couldn't explain my x-rays. The first ones clearly showed that the bullet had cut my spinal cord and lodged right alongside it, but the ones taken just last night seemed to portray a different story. He planned to take more x-rays to be sure, but if the results continued to show that the cord was intact, he would recommend that I have surgery as soon as possible to have the bullet removed. How could the bullet move? Was this some kind of miracle? Maybe all the prayers were having some impact. But could prayer really effect such a radical change? Dr. Lolley later showed me the x-ray pictures, and the early ones appeared to be distinctly different from those taken after the second day.

My spinal cord not being severed was good news, but I really hadn't thought much about the spinal injury and its implications, and I didn't relish further surgery at the moment. Nevertheless, I would do whatever Dr. Lolley thought best. When I next talked to my parents, they had already received the same report directly from Dr. Lolley. They didn't seem to be as sure about my having the operation as I was. I didn't know that the doctor had warned them more graphically than he had me about the danger of the surgery.

Late the next morning, Dr. Lolley came by to tell me that the x-rays continued to look good and that he would arrange the operation as soon as it could be done. Another doctor would do this surgery.

I found out sometime on Friday that the operation would be early Monday morning. During the daily group rounds with the interns, Dr. Lolley told them of the plans, and one of them asked why the operation wasn't going to be Saturday. He thought the likelihood of permanent paralysis was increased the longer the bullet remained lodged against my spinal cord. Dr. Lolley didn't question his logic; he merely said that one doctor doesn't second-guess another. In years to come, I would wonder what the results might have been if the operation had been performed a couple of days sooner.

That night a young aide who was attending to me asked, "Are you worried about your operation on Monday morning?" I replied something to the effect that I was not, and then bluntly he asked, "You know you might not make it, don't you?"

It was his next question that I would really dwell on over the weekend. Hesitantly he asked, "Are you afraid to die?"

CHAPTER THREE

I did a lot of reflecting and soul-searching as I stared into the very real face of death. As I lay there and carefully reviewed the development of my beliefs and faith, here is what I discovered:

I had always considered myself a religious person. I had been raised in a devout Southern Baptist home where we were expected to and did go to church every Sunday. I was still a member of a Baptist church and believed strongly in most of the theology which it taught. There were questions, however, for which formal religion, as I knew it, appeared to have no answers. Why are some people born with so many advantages and others with virtually no hope of achievement? What about people born with or who experience terrible physical or mental handicaps? We obviously don't enter this world with equal opportunities nor do we experience the same number and kind of trials in life. This apparent inequality and injustice had always bothered me. I simply was told not to question God's will and to take everything on faith—whatever that meant.

In addition, from my earliest childhood recollections, there had been a background of experiences with which I seemed to be vaguely and fleetingly familiar. As a youngster, I could sometimes relate whatever was happening to those very early feelings and vague remembrances. These haunting memories, if they could actually be called that, seemed to predate my present life. From school age on, they occurred less often and were less compelling, but occasionally something would happen and stir those memories that were surely outside the cognizance of this lifetime.

Then, years later, this mystery resurfaced. Ken, my fraternity brother in college, occasionally hypnotized members of our fraternity. It was funny to watch them do strange things under hypnosis, such as get "drunk" on water, which they had been told was bourbon. Several took their shoes off for no good reason after they had been told they would do so when they woke up.

One day, Ken took Joe back to the date of his birth. Joe told of his first sensations upon entering this world and gave the names of the attending doctor and two nurses at the hospital. (After awakening, Joe had no idea whether these names were correct, but later checked with his mother and learned they were exactly right.) Ken asked Joe to go back in time to just before his birth, and Joe described what appeared to be the womb environment. Then Ken told Joe it was two weeks before his birth and that he should tell us what he saw. Slowly and hesitantly, Joe described a pastoral scene of some beauty and said that he was getting ready to leave there and move into the earth's plane to be born. It had been a place he enjoyed and one he was very reluctant to leave, but had recognized it as a duty to move on. He had friends there which included relatives of his (in this life) who had died before he was born.

Then Ken surprised everyone witnessing the regression. He asked Joe to go back to the year 1900 and tell what he saw. The date didn't seem to have any significance to Joe, so Ken took him to the year 1800. Joe began mumbling rather incoherently, and Ken asked him to speak louder.

"I'm in the cotton field," Joe replied rather matter-of-factly. His voice was high pitched.

"What is your name?"

"Melinda. But they all call me 'Mindy.'"

"Are you a girl?"

"Of course," Joe laughingly replied.

"Where do you live?"

"On the plantation."

Joe's last answer was given as though everyone would know where the plantation was. Further questioning eventually revealed that Mindy lived near Savannah, Georgia, and was a black slave. She had lived a rather sheltered and hard life, dying in her twenties during childbirth soon after the year 1800.

We were all stunned. This kind of thing was new to most of us, although a few had heard of Bridey Murphy, a name currently in the news because of hypnotic past-life claims. Ken then went to the year 1850 and asked Joe what he saw. Joe began describing a house that seemed to be his home.

"Where is this house and do you live there?" Ken asked.

"Yes, in Bowling Green."

"Bowling Green, Kentucky?"

"Yes."

I became even more interested in what Joe was saying now because I had grown up near Bowling Green and had been there many times.

"What is the name of the street you live on?"

"Cherry Street," Joe answered after a short pause.

Ken went on to obtain his name and other details of his life in Bowling Green in 1850. As I recall, Joe claimed to have been a cabinetmaker then. I took notes on what he was saying. Finally, Joe said he died in the late 1860s and was buried in a country cemetery "at the Goshen Church on the Russellville Pike."

After awakening, Joe was as surprised as everyone else at what we told him he had said. He had never in his current life been to Georgia or Bowling Green, Kentucky. Joe had grown up in Cynthiana, Kentucky, at least 100 miles from Bowling Green.

Ken hypnotized others with similar results. Everyone described past lives, no matter how opposed they were in their conscious state to such a concept. Ken tried unsuccessfully to hypnotize me. I wanted to be hypnotized but found there was a little bit of me that was fighting "going under." I determined, however, to take my "Joe notes" home with me during the upcoming Christmas vacation and go to Bowling Green to see if I could verify the details Joe had given under hypnosis.

I found that checking into this kind of information from a century or more before isn't easy. I couldn't locate birth and death records that went back that far. The family name that Joe had given wasn't too common, but I found a number of people by that name who now lived in Bowling Green. There was a Cherry Street that had apparently been around for many years, although most of the homes were fairly modern. The church where he claimed to have been buried, on the Russellville Pike, was no longer there, but there was an old cemetery and there had once been such a church. Unfortunately, there were no names on gravestones prior to the year 1870. Before that, there were simply sandstone markers whose names, if ones had ever been written upon them, were now weathered away. By and large, I was impressed with how much general information I was able to verify. How could Joe have known what he did about life in Bowling Green if he had never been there? He was able to give information before his present birth just as easily—and seemingly as accurately—as he could retrieve incidents from this life which were no longer a part of his conscious memory.

I began to suspect that we all really have been here before and have had a variety of experiences. My suspicions were enhanced by a tour of active duty with the air force in

North Africa and Europe in 1958 and 1959.

I was sent from Wheelus air base at Tripoli, Libya, where I was stationed, to an air force tax conference at Pisa, Italy. (Being a legal officer in the armed services, I needed to be able to give current and accurate tax information to our military personnel and their dependents.) Italy really captured my fancy. After the conference, I took two or three days of leave to join a tour group and went to Naples and the Isle of Capri before returning to Libya. On the way to Naples, we stopped at an outdoor restaurant along the waterfront. Immediately behind us was a large cliff, and, while eating, I spied the ruins of an old temple on top of the cliff. I was inundated with powerful feelings of identity and recollection of that temple or one like it. It was an emotional experience that stayed with me for days.

Even more powerful were my feelings on a trip to Athens and Istanbul. When I came out of my hotel in Athens in the evening, I saw the lighted Acropolis hill and the hauntingly beautiful stone ruins of the Parthenon. I could barely control my emotions; I wanted to shout with joy; I had to fight tears. Everywhere I went around Athens that evening, I had the feeling of returning home. I even knew what I would see at some of the sites along the self-guided tour route before I got there.

Then in Turkey, some of the early Byzantine Christian churches in and around Istanbul (formerly Constantinople) brought on strong, although vague, memories. I was sure I had been a part of that early Christian effort.

In more recent years, I had even tried my own hand at hypnotism. I studied hypnotic techniques and joined the Kentucky Hypnosis Society. A friend had told me of a high school student of hers who was extremely psychic and wanted to be hynotically regressed. I agreed to work with him. Skip was an excellent subject and, in time, gave copious details of more than twenty alleged past lives, including one as a passing trader who witnessed the crucifixion of Jesus.

Another friend, Sam, had been a Catholic priest for a time in the 1960s and was still struggling with his religious convictions, although he remained staunchly Christian. He asked me to hypnotize him and tape record what transpired. Under hypnosis, he described a life as a member of the monastic religious faction, the Essenes, at the time of Jesus. He had heard both John the Baptist and Jesus speak and was able to give graphic accounts of their discourses. I asked him if he believed Jesus was the messiah and was surprised at his reply.

"We have studied Him carefully and conclude He is not the messiah we were expecting. We had hoped He was."

"Why did you decide He is not?" I cautiously asked.

"The scriptures and law talk of a priestly messiah, a kingly messiah, as well as a suffering messiah. He is not a king, and, since he is not a Levite, he is not a priest."

Although I had learned that the most unexpected information can surface under hypnosis and that subjects aren't just trying to please the conductor or say what is expected, I still was a little stunned at his answer. I knew that historically Jesus hadn't been openly and universally embraced by the Essenes as the promised messiah, but I was surprised at Sam's rationale for why they hadn't. Years later, I read in a book on the Dead Sea Scrolls, which are generally thought to have been the property and product of the Essenes, that there was information in them about expectations for a priestly, kingly, and suffering messiah.

How could Sam have known such details if he hadn't, in fact, lived as an Essene—as he claimed under hypnosis? It hadn't been wish fulfillment on his part, for he had been astonished and even bothered by what he had heard when I replayed the tape recording for him. On the other hand, it is impossible to prove from these hypnotic regressions that we have actually lived past lives, especially to the skeptic. On one occasion, however, I was able to put the possibility of past lives to practical application.

A married couple, both of whom were my good friends, came to me with an unusual request. They were experiencing personality problems which they couldn't understand. They wanted me to regress the wife and see if there were any past-life experiences that might explain their difficulties. I urged them to go to a professional counselor for such a regression, but they said they trusted me and no one else. We all three prayed about the situation; finally I agreed to see what might happen.

As soon as she was in a hypnotic trance, we went back in time, concentrating on any lifetimes in which they might have known each other. There were two or three, but eventually we got to ancient Egypt, and she seemed to be rather emotional about that lifetime together. They were lovers then, but he ended up having her killed. I tried to get her to talk about the situation as much as she would, and then I told her to forgive him for what he had done. I gave further directions that she would be able now in this lifetime to let go of this memory in complete forgiveness and that nothing from that lifetime would impede their love for each other now.

When she was awakened, she claimed to feel much better, and they went home feeling that they better understood why there had been personality problems. Some months later, they told me that their relationship had greatly improved. Now a few years later, they are still happily married.

Everything seemed to point to the reality of reincarnation, but how could I fit reincarnation into my traditional Christian background? I didn't have the answer, so I tried to avoid the question. I lost interest in going to church. None of the churches seemed to address the issues that were important to me. I didn't discontinue a spiritual search; I just couldn't find any sources that provided the answers for which I was seeking. Then in 1968 I ran into the psychic material of Edgar Cayce.

My introduction to Cayce was the best-selling book, *Edgar Cayce—The Sleeping Prophet,* by Jess Stearn. An attorney for one of the other Farm Credit banks suggested that I would enjoy reading the book. He and I had gone through some long philosophical and religious discussions together. He finally brought Jess Stearn's book to me and practically forced me to read it. It had the answers I was seeking. Information given by Cayce in trance affirmed my basic religious beliefs as well as those regarding past lives. From then on, I read everything I could about Edgar Cayce and the subject of reincarnation. I was surprised how much there was on this latter subject and how many great minds had believed in it. Surprisingly, reincarnation wasn't just an Eastern mystical concept but had been an important part of some branches of early Christianity as well.

Actually, I remembered having run into Edgar Cayce's name three years before. I had been doing some remodeling on my apartment building and had the radio playing in the background as I worked. At one point, I got interested in the story being told on an NBC radio "Monitor Series" about a miracle man in Virginia Beach, Virginia. He had given information while in trance which had healed people from many illnesses. What's more, from that radio program it sounded like Cayce also answered some of the philosophical questions that had been troubling me. At the end of the program, the name and address of the organization carrying on Cayce's work had been given, and I had stopped and written it down. For some inexplicable reason, I had never followed through on it.

Even further back in time, when I was about seven years old and while visiting relatives in Bowling Green, Kentucky, I had heard of Cayce. However, I didn't remember the name nor make the connection until many years later when I read another book on Cayce, *There Is a River,* by Thomas Sugrue. Being only seven, I wasn't allowed to participate in many adult activities, but my relatives were playing a card game which they, to my delight, allowed me to join. It was a loud, boisterous game in which the players shouted the number of cards they wanted to trade. Commodities, such as corn, wheat, and oats, were depicted on the cards that were traded. The object was to be the first to corner all the cards of a particular commodity through the trading. I remember someone remarking that the inventor of the game had lived in Bowling Green. Someone else added that he was a strange and unusual man who did unbelievable things. I had learned in recent books that the inventor of the card game—called Pit—had been Edgar Cayce.

My thrill in finding the Cayce material was heightened by the fact that he had been born and had lived for a number of years in the general area of my home in western Kentucky. My sister even lived in his hometown of Hopkinsville, and I began running into people who had known him when he was in Kentucky in the early part of this century. He had moved to Virginia Beach in the 1920s and died there in 1945, but the material in his stenographi-cally recorded psychic readings, given for thousands of inquiring individuals, answered the questions that had plagued me for years.

Cayce's psychic readings, as I came to learn more about them, supported the basic concepts that were a part of my Christian beliefs but added other insights as well. They claimed that each soul is eternal and has lived many life-times in an odyssey of its return to God, from whom all souls originally came. It was in the misuse of our soul's free will that we had become lost in materiality and thus separated from God. Life is continuous, however, and the time spent on earth is for the purpose of learning right behavior and regaining our lost paradise with God. Suddenly, biblical stories, such as creation and the prodigal son, took on new meaning. Most important for me, however, was the opportunity for melding my religious convictions with those of reincarnation. From that point on, my life and its direction took a new bent. The key, according to Cayce, for the return journey to the Father—or heaven—is to eliminate selfishness in one's life through love and service to others, just as Jesus had done. I had become alive with the excitement of life's purpose and potential.

Cayce had said what I wanted to believe, but was I being naive in accepting these concepts so quickly? They had an inner ring of truth for me, but I still needed some kind of testing. So I decided to try one of the strange bits of health advice Cayce had given to see if it would work for me. He said that we become susceptible to the common cold germ when our bodies get "out of balance" by being overly alkaline or overly acid, especially acid. He recommended taking two or three drops of Glyco-Thymoline in a glass of water daily to maintain a balance between alkalinity and acidity. Glyco-Thymoline was a popular mouthwash in his time and is still available today. I tried this simple "treatment" and virtually eliminated colds from my life. Previously, I had always had two or three every year.

Now that I felt I had the answers for which I had been searching, I was sure others would also welcome the Cayce insights. To my utter amazement, some friends reacted with abject horror. They were sure that I had turned to witchcraft or the devil himself. On a visit with my mother, I excitedly related my discoveries of psychic information—and reincarnation in particular. She accepted the psychic bit; she had had some ESP experiences herself. But she was appalled at my interest in reincarnation.

"You mean we may come back as an animal?" she queried.

I assured her that the Cayce information—and a lot of other sources—insisted that humans come back only as humans. The material I was studying didn't support transmigration of souls, the theory my mother was mistakenly equating with reincarnation. The kind of person we are in the next life, of course, may depend on what we have done with the present life, but we don't sink into lower life forms.

"But reincarnation is against the Bible," Mother insisted.

I pointed out what were to me biblical references to reincarnation, including the statement Jesus made to His disciples that Elijah had returned as John the Baptist (Matthew 17:10-13). She wasn't convinced.

Sometimes, however, I had been surprised at the interest and positive response I received. Several friends at work were as excited as I at the Cayce concepts. I had told Donnie about the hypnotic regression with Skip, in which he claimed to have witnessed the crucifixion. The tape recording of the session was very moving and powerful, and he borrowed it and listened to it. To my surprise, he invited me on Easter Sunday to come to his rural Baptist church and play it. They responded to it quite positively and asked me to come back again. You could just never know how people would respond and what they might be seeking.

The Cayce material had for me truly put a premium on service to my fellow human beings and the avoidance of pursuits that were primarily selfish. I was glad that my work was service-oriented, and I felt comfortable in my job of dispensing agricultural credit to farmers in the area. As president of the bank, I had many opportunities to speak to groups and gently weave some of the Cayce philosophy and insights into speeches and conversation, although I never spoke directly of reincarnation. The principles were consistently received with enthusiasm by audiences who didn't know the source of the ideas.

One talk in particular stands out in my mind. In Nashville, Tennessee, I wove in quotes from Cayce about the spiritual value of getting close to the soil and of the life force in all living things, including plants. Afterward, I was beseiged by members of the audience, all of whom had farm and agricultural backgrounds; they had been entranced with the scope and potential of these thoughts. This experience powerfully reinforced my feeling that Cayce was right about one idea especially: No one finds oneself where he or she is by accident. For me that meant two things: (1) At a personal level, I could bring new spiritual insights to others through my profession; and (2) at a universal level everything has a purpose and opportunity; all we have to do is make the most of it. I failed often, of course, but felt that I now had an ideal toward which to strive, knew what I was supposed to do, and was in a perfect place to do it.

This philosophy had been very helpful to me when I had first awakened at the hospital and become aware of my predicament. Although there had been some inevitable questions of why this tragedy had happened, I thought I recognized the hand of God in the strange sequence of events which had insured my survival. If I had been spared, then there must be something purposeful remaining for me to do. All of this helped buoy me with a feeling of optimism and hope which surprised many with whom I had come in contact.

I remembered a rather strange feeling in the hours just before being shot. After I had left an employee dinner and meeting at Martin Bonar's apartment, it seemed that the evening moonlight on the two-day-old snow was unusually bright and beautiful. I was acutely aware of how lucky I was to have my position working with such fine employees and in such an enjoyable and rewarding job. Over and over again as I headed home, I said prayers of thanksgiving. For the rest of my conscious minutes that evening, I was on a unique emotional high, full of gratitude for all my blessings.

Maybe my higher consciousness was doing something to prepare me for what lay ahead.

In the hospital, I had learned that when Tom called the police that night, there luckily had been a cruiser nearby. When the police asked Tom what hospital they should take me to, he had suggested General Hospital when he had meant to name another one. As it turned out, only General Hospital had the facilities to save my life. Dr. Lolley had said I was within five minutes of death when he stopped my internal bleeding. I learned later that he was the only doctor within 300 miles who had performed the kind of surgery I required. Why had he been on duty and available that night at General? How had the bullet, according to the x-rays, changed positions in my back? Surely all these things hadn't happened by accident nor for the purpose that on Monday morning I would die on the operating table.

Yet, even if it were destined that I should not survive the coming surgery, I was convinced of the continuation of the life of the soul and the wisdom of God's will. I prayed the prayer of Jesus in Gethsemane with a fervor and conviction I had never experienced before: "Father, not my will, but Thine be done."

I recalled psychic readings by Edgar Cayce on life and death, and they helped dispel any possible fears. They said:

> For there is no death, to those who love the Lord; only the entering into God's other chamber . . .
>
> It is not the end, then, because we pass from one room to another, from one consciousness to another.
>
> 2282-1

> For, life is of the Creator—and it may only be changed, it *cannot* be ended or destroyed. It can *only* return from whence it came.   497-1

In addition, I had come to believe that I had been through

the death experience numerous times before—and "survived."

I had joined a Search for God study group some three years before. They met each Sunday evening in my home. Such groups had grown out of a series of psychic readings given by Cayce to a small group decades earlier. Members of this group had asked how they could become more spiritual and psychic, and in trance Cayce had given them answers through numerous readings over a period of eleven years. The material was recorded and put into two small books which groups, such as mine and over a thousand others world-wide, studied and tried to apply in their individual lives.

The word "group" may for some conjure up erroneous connotations. But the format of a Search for God group is based on several persons who commit to a spiritual search together. The ten or so members of my group had learned that simple traits, such as cooperation, patience, fellowship, and love, are essential ingredients of the spiritual recipe. In the intimacy of the group setting, we were forced to deal with these traits in the process of relating to each other— sometimes under extreme and intensely challenging circumstances. It seemed, however, that those who weren't ready for such a journey soon dropped out and that others who were ready had found their way to the group at the appropriate time. The ultimate goal and crowning achievement would, it is hoped, be a deep, abiding, *agape* love for each person—not just among group members, but with all souls everywhere.

As I lay there in my hospital bed on the weekend before the operation, I remembered a sentence in the "Patience" lesson our group had studied shortly before. It had troubled me at the time, stating: "He that is without crosses has ceased to be of notice and is no longer among the sons [of God]." (*A Search for God*, Book I, A.R.E. Press, Virginia Beach,

Va., 1942, 1970, p. 82) Life had gone so smoothly and nicely for me at the time that I had wondered if God had given up on me. There had actually been a feeling of relief and comfort in the hospital that first day when I remembered the above statement and recognized in the events that had transpired the possibility that God was aware of my existence, for God had given me a very real cross to bear. Subsequent events also suggested He was looking after my welfare. A Cayce reading promised:

> For His grace *is* sufficient unto the end. He that endureth the cross shall wear the crown; not he that gives up, that cries "Enough" and is ready to quit, but they that press on even when there apparently is no way out.   303-6

I was determined to weather my current crisis with as much optimism, courage, and faith as I could possibly muster.

So for me, past formal religion and the Cayce information, including the study group experience, were all invaluable in preparing me for my present situation. Throughout the weekend, I reviewed my beliefs and realized that I could accept whatever happened with a genuine faith in its ultimate rightness.

When Monday morning arrived, when my parents came by for a last-minute visit, when the nurses and technicians prepared me for the operation and rolled me to the operating room, I was calm, tranquil, and confident. I was even joking with the nurses and rather enjoying the experience. Such a cavalier attitude truly surprised me. I concluded it must be attributed to a force and power beyond myself, of which I had never been fully aware until now and which previously hadn't been so genuinely tested.

CHAPTER FOUR

The next thing I remember was someone telling me to wake up because the mayor's wife was on her way. I regained consciousness fairly quickly and was surprised to learn that the surgery was over and that the bullet had been removed. The volunteer nurse attending to me was very nice. It turned out she lived close to my home and was a friend of Mayor Harvey Sloane and his wife, Kathy. The nurse was to tell me that Kathy would be there early in the morning to greet me in the recovery room. It was actually the next day before Kathy would get there, but the expectation of her visit and her final arrival caused quite a stir among the hospital staff. I think I may have gotten a little extra attention because of the celebrity visit.

For twenty-four hours, I wasn't even allowed to raise my head. I think it was because of the anesthesia I had received during the operation. All I could remember of the operation was what seemed to be a dream in which I was on the west coast in California. I was by the ocean, at the edge of and just about to fall off the continent. I also had seemed to be a blob of putty continually being reshaped and reformed. I don't know what, if anything, the dream meant. Maybe I was on the edge of life about to take on a new form of existence. If I had been close to death in either this surgery or just after the shooting, I hadn't had one of the now-famous "near-death experiences." While I may have been close to death the night of the shooting, I don't think I ever was clinically dead.

I was relieved that the operation was over and that the bullet had now been removed. The pain in my legs was as bad as ever, but I reasoned that it was because of the surgery and that it would go away with the healing that was sure to follow.

My parents were still allowed to visit me in the recovery room (actually, I was in a side wing of the recovery area), but other than their brief visits and an occasional one from a doctor or nurse, I was totally alone in the room. Time seemed to drag on interminably.

By the second day, I was begging the doctor and nurses to get me back to the Intensive Care Unit. It was funny; I never thought I would want to go back there, but Intensive Care sounded awfully good at the moment. If I needed any kind of attention now, it would sometimes take an hour or more before a nurse or aide would arrive. The problem of moving me seemed to be that there was no empty bed in the ICU. Finally, with the help of the nurse who was a friend of the Sloanes, I got back to the ICU on the third day after surgery. The nurses and aides there, whom I'd gotten to know earlier, seemed like long-lost family with whom I was being reunited.

Life now took on a routine and regularity which wasn't altogether pleasant but which nevertheless was welcomed. I knew when visitors were arriving, when the doctors would make their rounds, when the nurses would perform their various duties, and the occurrences of all the other activities that are part of hospital existence. At least these rhythms helped the time to pass and gave me a sense of progression.

The doctor who had removed the bullet told me that everything had gone well during the operation. The bullet was a 32-caliber and had been turned over to the police. The spinal nerve cord hadn't been severed but was badly bruised. He mentioned that it was possible for me to get some recovery from the paralysis, but there was no assurance that that would happen. I think he said the odds were about 50 percent. If the pain continued and was too severe, another operation might be necessary to actually sever the nerves. But he wanted to wait a year before making that decision. It would be years before anyone would mention that option again.

Although I had been anxious to return to the ICU, at times it was an unbelievably difficult ordeal. One of the other patients, an older black man, was also suffering from a gunshot wound, and he moaned, shook, and carried on all night long every night. I found out later that his behavior was the result of alcohol withdrawal and that I was witnessing a classic case of delirium tremens.

During the weekend, a number of doctors spent hours working with an electronic heart pacemaker on the patient next to me. They couldn't get it to work, and I know the patient must have been suffering greatly as wires protruded through the skin while the doctors manipulated controls on the little box to which the wires were attached. Late Saturday afternoon, three of the doctors left and said to the remaining doctor, an intern from India, "You believe in reincarnation; maybe you can bring him back to life." The poor patient spent most of the night with the wires sticking out from a gaping hole near his heart. He disappeared the next day, and I assumed he hadn't survived. It certainly was a most unpleasant environment in which to be recuperating.

One day Dr. Lolley introduced me to a new doctor; his name was Kelley. He was an expert on rehabilitating patients with nerve injuries. His questions and pin-pricking examination of my body were quite a production; the only thing lacking was music and spotlights, as he made his checks and rattled into his tape recorder diagnoses and words that were unintelligible to me. Finally, he said I would probably be a patient of his soon.

Shortly thereafter, a young man stopped by to visit and said he was a hospital volunteer. He indicated he also did volunteer work at the Institute of Physical Medicine and Rehabilitation and that he understood I would probably be going there in a few more weeks. He told me not to be intimidated by Dr. Kelley's manner, but that I would get to know him and like him in the days ahead if I chose to go to his rehabilitation center. He urged me to opt for this treatment because it would greatly speed my recovery. I never saw him again, but I genuinely appreciated his visit and words of encouragement.

One nurse was insistent that I sit up in a chair. It took ten minutes for her and a couple of aides to get me and my tubes and equipment moved to a chair by the bed. The pain was excruciating. I could tell by the looks on the faces of my visiting parents and Walter Brown, my predecessor as bank president, that they weren't impressed by my performance. Fifteen minutes was all the time I could stand out of bed. I recognized anew the long road of recovery which lay ahead.

By this time, I was ready to take nourishment on my own, rather than through the IV tubes. Dr. Lolley agreed that I could have liquids by mouth. Juice, jello, and clear soups tasted like ambrosia. After two days of such nourishment, the doctors said that my electrolytes, or something I didn't understand, weren't measuring up to what was considered normal. On the doctor-intern rounds that afternoon, one young intern insisted to Dr. Lolley that I should be taken off liquids by mouth until this situation improved. I begged to be allowed to continue with the oral liquid food, but Dr. Lolley ruled against me.

The next three or four days were some of the most agonizing that I would experience. I was hungry on top of all the other pain and problems, continually fantasizing about food or water. Occasionally they would let me sip on an ice cube. I couldn't get my mind away from dishes of various foods or scenes of nature where there was running water. It was winter and cold outside; I kept visualizing melting ice, crystal clear streams, and waterfalls.

There was an area in southeastern Kentucky for which I had developed a fond affection because of its rugged beauty: cliffs, clear streams, waterfalls, and, above all, beautiful emerald-green Lake Cumberland. This area had become my vacationland in recent years, and I often went boating there during the summer months. There was a spiritual quality about the scenery in the area, and my trips there were like a visit to Mecca, always seeming to have a rejuvenating effect. I kept picturing myself there among the thousands of hidden coves and spots of majestic natural beauty. I think these mental excursions were actually therapeutic, and they certainly helped to take my mind off the pain and hunger.

I frequently pictured one particular spot. In Daniel Boone National Forest, near the far end of the South Fork of Lake Cumberland and the Cumberland River, a special waterfall had captured my fancy. It was called Yahoo Falls. There were very few visitors because not many people knew of its existence. Trails had been built to it in the 1930s by WPA workers, and they had been maintained by the U.S. Forest Service since then. A thin, eighty-foot stream of water poured over the face of a cliff, behind which was a natural "cave" or eroded area. It was thus easy to walk behind the falls and observe it from many perspectives. The waterfall ended in a small, tranquil pool, from which a stream flowed for about a quarter of a mile before entering Lake Cumberland. The surrounding cliffs, virtually virgin forest, and other features made this spot one of incredible serenity and beauty. In my bed at General Hospital I vowed that I would someday return there. I would love to show this spot to others—maybe my study group friends who had come to be so important in my life and who would be even more so in the months ahead.

After two or three days, Dr. Lolley finally heeded my pleadings and said I could have liquid food again. The problem wasn't quite resolved, but he decided to gamble. I cannot describe my elation, and for the next two days—that is, the remainder of my stay in the ICU and General Hospital—I again enjoyed jello and clear broths. There were no undesirable effects, and my electrolyte measurements gradually returned to acceptable levels.

I was again transferred to a chair, this time a wheelchair, and rolled out of the ICU. Finally we reached a window in the hallway, and for the first time in nearly two weeks, I could see the outside world. I never dreamed the skyline of Louisville, a typical American medium-sized metropolitan city, could look so appealing.

My condition had improved sufficiently, and I was taken off the "critical" list, which meant leaving the ICU. I began pleading with Dr. Lolley to get me to another hospital and not send me to the general ward, about which I had heard so many unpleasant stories.

My timing, however, seemed to be wrong. For the first time in months, all the other hospitals were filled; there was no empty bed in town. But finally late the next day, Dr. Lolley said there was an opening at Norton Hospital, a new building one block away, and I quickly agreed to the change. It was early evening when I finally was rolled to an ambulance and transported to Norton. I was exhausted after the transfer but felt that a major milestone had been reached.

I found saying good-by to Dr. Lolley unexpectedly difficult. He had saved my life. Without him, I would be dead. I liked his easygoing, positive manner. He was the epitome of what I thought a doctor should be, and we had gotten along remarkably well. I had never before been indebted to anyone for saving my life. My voice was emotional as I thanked him for what he had done.

He then gave me a fatherly talk. He told me he had helped write medical history with me and that I had been a good patient. This last statement surprised me; I felt that I had been too impatient and had consistently been pushing the staff. He encouraged me, however, to keep this aggressive and positive attitude, for I was "not yet out of the woods." In fact, there was a long way still to go, and I would have to work like I never had before. He told me to keep pushing just as I had, for food, a better hospital—for all the things that I thought had been a nuisance for him. I didn't then realize how difficult it is to recover if one has an attitude of malaise and apathy. I would see many examples of it around me in the days and months ahead.

There were tears in my eyes as I shook Dr. Lolley's hand for the last time. He was waving as the ambulance pulled away.

CHAPTER FIVE

Life at Norton Hospital was like that of an entirely different world. Everything was brand new, and all the rooms were private. I had television and visitors galore. The bank where I worked was only two blocks away, and my friends made up for lost time in visiting. Even one of the nurses in the hospital turned out to be a high school friend and grade school sweetheart whom I hadn't seen in over twenty years. Barbara and I recalled the fun we had together in our high-school junior-class drama playing lovers. As I looked around me and my new environment, I had difficulty adjusting to such regal conditions.

I quickly was reminded, however, of my personal condition and limitations. As much as I enjoyed the visitors, I soon tired and sometimes yearned for a few minutes of solitude to rest and recover. I noticed, too, for the first time how much violence and gunplay are on television. I became mentally distraught whenever someone was shot or threatened by a gun. This reaction surprised me because I couldn't actually remember ever seeing a gun or feeling threatened when I was shot. Our brain apparently stores more of our experiences than we realize—even those memories of which we aren't normally conscious.

I had a new physician who had been selected by Dr. Lolley. He, too, was excellent, but each of his visits was an ordeal. Although all of the tubes into my body were now gone, there was an opening just below my right chest. Though bandaged, it allowed drainage of the yet continuing internal bleeding. (I found out later that this hole was where the bullet had entered.) Each day the doctor inserted a metal object into this opening and spread it apart so that it wouldn't heal shut too quickly and stop the flow of what was apparently necessary drainage. The pain was excruciating.

My first full day at Norton was spectacular. The doctors said I could now eat solid foods. It was my fortieth birthday, and by hospital custom birthdays permitted a special meal. I will always remember that dinner of beef-tomato soup, steak, salad, vegetables, and chocolate cake. The soup was extraordinary, and I savored every sip. But after having had no real food for two weeks, the rest of the meal was more than I could handle. However, I did manage a taste of the cake.

The next day, I was put on a special low-calorie, non-calcium diet. I was sure there had been some mistake; my doctor said he hadn't ordered it. But the restrictive fare continued, and I later learned it was on the orders of Dr. Kelley from the rehabilitation center. How did he get into the picture? I wasn't really his patient yet, or was I? I couldn't keep up with all my doctors and specialists.

Shortly after I arrived, a woman came by to start my physical rehabilitation. It began with minor exercises. She also ordered a special wheel arrangement to which I was periodically fastened and rotated in a complete circle above my bed. It was something like a ferris wheel, but my pain was greatly increased while "riding" on it. It was necessary, she said, for me to be rotated in this fashion in order to change body positions from the perpetual reclining position of the bed.

One evening after the regular x-ray, the nurse said I had

pneumonia, and new medication was given to me. Even though I didn't feel any worse, my spirits took a nose-dive. It would be another twenty-four hours before the problem of misdiagnosis was straightened out. The technician who read my x-ray failed to observe from my chart that I had received an injury to my right lung and mistook the injury spot for evidence of infectious pneumonia. I wished all my problems would go away so easily!

I was in Norton Hospital for a week. My doctor had concluded he could now stop the painful daily wound opening, and I was elated. He asked if I wanted to go to Dr. Kelley's rehabilitation center. I told him I would leave it to his best judgment. The next thing I knew, I was being transported one block away, back within sight of General Hospital, to the rehabilitation center. This would be my home for many weeks to come.

CHAPTER SIX

My poor timing continued. I arrived at the Institute of Physical Medicine and Rehabilitation at 1:00 p.m., just as they had directed. The patient whose place I was taking, however, hadn't vacated. For a couple of hours, I was left on a rolling stretcher in the dining area until he left and the bed was ready for me. They did give me a cup of orange sherbet while I was waiting, and it tasted unusually good. My hands were free, but otherwise I was tied down and unable to move. My leg pains seemed to get worse when I remained in the same position for any period of time, and I began to really suffer. When I finally got to my new bed, I was exhausted but happy to have a place to lie down, even though I couldn't leave it or even turn without help from someone else.

The rehab center was connected to Jewish Hospital by a second-floor walkway and used some of its services. The center could accommodate some thirty patients and had acquired a good reputation in medical circles for its management and rehabilitative work. I was not quite sure then but soon came to realize it was where I should be.

All the patients had some form of paralysis. The Institute's goal was to retrain and restrengthen muscles and to teach patients to become more adept in their new, restricted life style. A large part of the first floor consisted of a gym or workroom where physical exercise took place. There was also a room for occupational therapy, where, it was hoped, one could learn a new, but manageable income-producing job, as well as to perform simple household duties, such as cooking. The goal was for each patient to leave the Institute as self-sufficient as possible. There were doctors, nurses, aides, even a staff psychiatrist. The second floor consisted of patient rooms which could accommodate from one to four persons each.

I doubted that occupational therapy would have any value for me. As soon as I recovered, which would surely be achieved within a month or two, I would be back at my Farm Credit Bank and thus had no need to learn a new occupation. Domestic chores, such as cooking, had never been a talent of mine, but I would be able to get by as I had always done. I was totally optimistic about recovery and the future.

My roommate was a heavy-set black man who had been shot in the back with a shotgun during a quarrel over a traffic accident. He was in as bad a shape as I, and when I looked around during the evening group meal, I realized that was true for most of the patients. Some were even worse than I because they couldn't use their hands; they were quadraplegics. Everyone was required, if their physical condition possibly permitted, to eat meals together. Everyone had a wheelchair; those who couldn't navigate well were pushed into the dining room by staff aides.

In short order, I came to know the staff quite well. For the most part, they were dedicated and skilled at their jobs. One of the physical therapists had worked at my bank before going back to school for this training. Patty was stunned to see me in my present condition. I guess I still was, too. My personal physical therapist, Pam, was a very attractive young lady from St. Louis. She was quite professional but allowed and returned my lighthearted humor and banter.

We became good friends. The same was true for the nurses and aides; they knew and performed their job well but also had warm and loving personalities. They each took a real and personal interest in their patients. In a matter of weeks, they became almost as close to me as family.

I continued to have many visitors. One afternoon I looked up from my bed and saw Martha Binford enter the room. Martha was one of my Edgar Cayce study group friends. Although she wasn't in my group, it was her evident spiritual beauty and grace that had convinced me three years before to join a group. If I could become anything like her, it would be worth the commitment in time and effort for the weekly group meetings, I had reasoned to myself back then. Martha had joined a study group years before in Texas and had continued her group involvement in Kentucky while rearing a family of four girls. Her husband was a university professor who didn't share her interest in Edgar Cayce and study group work. He had died a few years before, and Martha stepped up her Cayce activity by becoming the Louisville area representative. I liked her patient, tolerant acceptance of everyone, regardless of where each one was on the spiritual path.

Martha told me of receiving a phone call about my shooting the night it had occurred. She had called the Association for Research and Enlightenment (A.R.E.), the Edgar Cayce membership organization in Virginia Beach, the next morning to put me on their worldwide prayer list. She said that my group members and others had spent the night on which I was shot praying for me. Maybe now I knew why so many miracles had occurred and why I was still alive with some hope of recovery.

Martha left a book with me which she said I might enjoy. It was Marcus Bach's *The World of Serendipity*. In the days ahead it truly focused my attitude in a more positive direction and challenged me to my best. Serendipity was defined as "the art of finding valuable or agreeable things not sought for" or discovering advantages in seeming adversity. This concept insisted there is a silver lining behind every cloud, and one has only to find it and harness it to be in charge of the forces of the universe. The story of Columbus was a classic example of serendipity—a man who failed to find a short route to India, but who instead discovered two new continents with wealth far surpassing that of India. Former Supreme Court Justice Benjamin Cardozo possibly has best described the process of serendipity:

> Like many of the finest things of life, like happiness and tranquillity and fame, the gain that is most precious is not the thing sought, but one that comes of itself in the search for something else. [Quoted in Marcus Bach's *The World of Serendipity* (DeVorss and Company, Marina del Ray, California, 1970), p. 8.]

It isn't that we fail to try. Quite the contrary: We need to go after what we think is good for us with all our zeal and vigor. But attachment to certain results must be avoided. Certainly we should hope for and expect what we desire. But if it doesn't happen, we must be ready to look for the better things that have come to us instead. Our expectation and prayer should always be for what is best, as only God can know and see it.

I was reminded of similar ideas in the Cayce readings:

> Then, do not count any condition lost. Rather make each the stepping-stone to higher things, remembering [that] God does not allow one to be tempted beyond that they are able to bear and comprehend, will they but make their will one with His.   900-44

We are encouraged to expect something unusual and

good from everything that happens to us.

> If the problems of the experience today, now, are taken as an expectancy for the unusual and that which is to be creative and hopeful and helpful, life becomes rather the creative song of the joyous worker. 1968-5

I wondered if there were possibly something good which could come out of my so-called tragedy. Would I come out of this experience better qualified to cope with whatever lay ahead? I wasn't sure, but at least I started thinking in terms of expectancy and hope. And I was determined that I wouldn't overlook whatever good fortune or new adventures might flow from my present adversity. This attitude, in and of itself, would turn out to be a very valuable treasure. It would encourage me to flow with and often profit from whatever came along. I started looking for the serendipitous opportunities that came with every activity, however unpleasant the circumstances might first appear to be.

Several times in the coming months, my study group concluded its regular Sunday evening meeting with a visit to my hospital room and a short meditation and prayer around my bed. Their concern and care for my welfare was very sustaining, and it was a contagious thing which affected others around me—patients and staff alike.

Another visitor about this time was Catherine Crabtree, one of my fellow study group members. She was an elegant woman, now in retirement, and a dear friend. I remember the first time she and Margie attended our group. They had been in another group for a time, one which met in the Louisville Library. I thought, as I listened to them talk about philosophical subjects, that they were too sophisticated to fit into our group. I soon found out that I was totally wrong in my hasty judgment. They had become solid pillars of our group and taught much to the rest of us.

I was pleased to see Catherine this particular day. Her first words were, "Well, you were told this was going to happen." I had no idea what she was talking about. "You remember your dream, don't you? It said it all."

I did remember telling my group the Sunday evening before my injury about a dream I had experienced the previous week. The fact that I had related the dream to them was unusual. Although we sometimes worked on dream interpretation and guidance in the group, I felt we often wasted a lot of time on such speculation and usually let others share their dreams if they desired, keeping mine to myself. But this dream had seemed very different and important, and I related it. No one seemed to have a good idea about its meaning that evening. It hadn't occurred to me in the interim that the dream had been prophetic in any way.

Here was the dream, as I had told it to the group:

I was driving in my car down a highway near an area of western Kentucky where I had grown up and first practiced law. Suddenly to my right, I realized I was passing a very beautiful city I had never seen before. It had a mystical, other-worldly quality, and I decided to stop and visit it. I had to back up my car to reach the road that led to it. As I drove on this side road and approached the city, I saw a bridge ahead. Before I reached the bridge, however, water covered the roadway, and my car stalled. The water seemed to be getting higher, and I urgently got out of my car and, to avoid drowning, waded back out of the water in the direction from which I had come and away from the beautiful city.

Catherine, who was good at dream interpretation, now explained to me the dream's meaning: I had deliberately chosen, in my unconscious mind, what had happened to me. At first, I went toward this city, which was symbolic of heaven, the other side, or life after death. I almost made it there, but the water, symbolizing spirituality, stopped me. I lost my means of transportation, that is, the car, which represented the actual loss of the use of my legs. I was able, however, to escape the rising waters and consequent death.

What she said seemed like a logical interpretation if, in fact, everything of importance that happens to us is first previewed in our higher consciousness through dreams. Cayce's psychic readings claim that this is exactly what occurs to us all, but I wasn't sure I was fully ready to accept this concept as fact. Certainly I had come close to death and had lost my normal means of transportation, my legs, which were now paralyzed. As time went on, however, I began to feel that the dream really had previewed the events that had happened. In the coming months, I had several dreams in which I eventually found my car again. At least these dreams and the way I interpreted them were helpful and promising. I hoped Catherine and Edgar Cayce knew what they were talking about.

I recalled also sometime later that for about a two-year period before being shot I had had a series of shooting-star dreams. They weren't dreams of falling stars, which might have hinted at sinister consequences, nor were they frightening. Rather, the vivid dreams were simply suggestive to me at the time of something major and important. In each dream, I was outside looking at the sky when a blazing ball of fire streaked across the heavens. In some of the dreams, I was back on the farm where I grew up; in others, I was in the Louisville area or at work. I wonder now if they might not have been a symbolic forecast of the shooting that lay ahead for me. I haven't had a shooting-star dream since then.

I was fast becoming convinced that there is much at work—in this universe *and* in our minds—about which we are only faintly aware and informed.

I soon fell into the routine of the rehab schedule. Twice a day I went downstairs to the exercise area and performed the exercises prescribed for me by my therapist, Pam. It was there that they first discovered I was beginning to get some return of feeling in my left leg. It was very slight, but it was something they could start to work with for muscle rehabilitation. From experience, Pam promised that the process would speed up as the muscles began to reacquire some strength. Nevertheless, the exercises and moving my leg were the hardest work I had ever had to do. Just wiggling my left toes exhausted me.

Very early I was measured for leg and body braces and told to pick out a wheelchair from catalogues that were available. I insisted that I didn't need a wheelchair; I expected to recover from my paralysis, and until then I planned to use the center's wheelchairs. I had told everyone from my office that I would be back there soon, and I fully expected to be. I certainly didn't anticipate needing a wheelchair there. As with many other things, I soon found that the rehab people knew more about the process of healing than I did.

The highlight of each week was Sunday morning when we could roll our wheelchairs into a shower area. By transferring to a stationary chair under the shower, we could get a welcome head-to-toe water cleansing. The greatest relief was a good hair shampooing; the hair gets oily and the scalp quite itchy after several days with one's head resting mostly in a pillow.

One Saturday evening, there was an unusually heavy procession of emergency vehicles at nearby General Hospital. I could tell by the sirens and flashing lights. The next day, I heard the story of how the car of a couple and their son was hit in downtown traffic by a drunken driver. One of the ambulances carrying the family to the hospital was then hit at an intersection by yet another vehicle driven by an intoxicated driver. The net result was the death of both parents and critical injury of the thirteen-year-old son. I had never known nor been privy to so much calamity and injury as had been my lot in the last two months. All around me were people who had suffered as much or more than I. At least this realization discouraged self-pity and the eternal questioning of "why me?"

The Board of Directors of my bank came to Louisville each month from the four states we served, and their meetings occurred around the middle of the month. In mid-February, they visited me at the rehab center. They were cheerful and positive, and I was encouraged by their attitude, although none of us had any idea when I would be back to work. They assured me everything was running smoothly despite my absence.

A month later, things were quite different. During their March meeting, three of the seven Board members came by and told me they were going to have to take some kind of action to replace me. They said the action wouldn't be effective until the end of March and offered me the opportunity to resign in the interim. I wasn't ready to admit an inability to resume my job as bank president but finally recognized I must bow to the Board's authority and accept their judgment. The next day, I asked my former secretary to come over for dictation, and I gave her a letter of resignation. Both of us had tears in our eyes during her brief visit.

Although I would later recognize that resignation was the best thing for me and the bank—and they were quite generous with me in severance benefits—I felt then that the Board had acted prematurely. I began to worry for the first time about my economic situation. What would I do even if I recovered fully? I had been totally engrossed in my job. I was fully satisfied with my position and had expected to be there until retirement. I had been able to use my legal background and my spiritual convictions to great advantage in the job. The people I had worked with were the salt of the earth. I was also pleased that I had moved so quickly to my present position; I was the youngest bank president in Farm Credit history. At thirty-nine, I had been elevated to a position which was considered for pay purposes comparable to a civil service presidential cabinet appointment. But now my whole world had totally collapsed.

I prepared a farewell letter to go to all the 1,200 or so people whom I worked with in the bank and in our associations. It was written from the heart:

March 25, 1974

TO ALL MY MANY FRIENDS:

I still can hardly believe the turn of events since January 8, 1974. On that evening, I left a dinner of Bank personnel at about 10:30, drove home, and showered. Hearing a cry for help from one of my tenants, I ran toward the doorway of the apartment and was shot by one of two fleeing intruders in the house. By 11:30, I was being admitted to the emergency ward of Louisville's General Hospital and was within five minutes of death from internal bleeding. Most of you know the story of the next few hours; the prayers of many of you, I am convinced, saved my life and effected what the doctors consider a miraculous recovery. The bullet, which had lodged in my spinal column, was removed a week later, but left me paralyzed pretty much from the waist down. Because my spinal cord had not been severed, however, the doctors held hope for some recovery of the paralyzed nerves.

The following days and weeks brought progress as well as a gradual recognition on my part of the seriousness and long-range implications of my condition. All of you, however, played a major role in keeping my morale within tolerable limits. There were so many, many examples of your thoughtfulness and consideration— such as the more than one thousand cards I have received. It is impossible to respond individually to all your good deeds, but I shall be eternally grateful to each of you.

Meanwhile, the important business of the Bank continued, and, although it was being ably handled by the fine Bank staff we are lucky to have, the need for designation of permanent leadership within the Bank became obvious. In consultation and collaboration with the District Board, I elected to resign from the Bank presidency and apply for disability retirement benefits. I have never done anything with more reluctance or regret. I am leaving a job I never dared expect to attain and a group of people whose quality cannot be duplicated anywhere. Throughout my nearly ten years with Farm Credit, and especially during my year as President, there was not a single PCA [Production Credit Association] that did not give me one hundred percent support and cooperation. For that I thank you from the bottom of my heart and trust you will do as much for my successor.

Recently, the two young men involved in my shooting were apprehended. One was a juvenile (seventeen years old) and was caught in the process of stealing a car. He confessed to a series of burglaries, robberies, and car thefts with his older partner (early twenties), on whom he put the primary blame and responsibility—including that for my shooting. Apparently, the shooting was a spur-of-the-moment happening when I ran between them and their route of retreat through the front door; they had intended to rob all three apartments in my building. The juvenile will probably receive a light or probated sentence, but the adult should receive a significant sentence on the charges.

I am learning to handle a wheelchair fairly well and gradually acquiring the knack of walking with braces and crutches. The doctors expect me to regain eventual control of my left leg, but use of my right leg below the knee is questionable. Looking to the future, I am not sure what kind of work I will be qualified for or interested in—anything else after Farm Credit will seem anticlimactical. I may be interested in doing some writing or charitable work if my financial situation permits. But, in any event, I am sure many of our paths will cross, and I look forward to each and every such occasion.

I leave Farm Credit with a heavy heart. I will miss rubbing elbows with all of you, and I regret not participating in the glorious future which I think is Farm Credit's destiny. I do, however, thank God for the wonderful years I shared in the System and the opportunity to have known each of you.

Sincerely,

The outpouring of goodwill and fond remembrances as a result of the letter was a tonic no doctor could prescribe nor pharmacist concoct.

I began to look ahead. I learned that I would receive monthly insurance disability benefit payments, which would be supplemented after six months by social security. My economic security was thus assured, but I couldn't imagine what my future would be like. Was my productive life over and would I be confined to a bed or wheelchair forever?

Then I remembered serendipity. There was surely a treasure or something of value to be found in the events of the last two months which had so drastically changed the direction of my life. All I had to do was look for it and not let it slip away unnoticed.

I recalled that Catherine, in her visit to tell me the meaning of my dream, said she had written Hugh Lynn Cayce, president of the A.R.E., suggesting I would be a good person for employment there. Before my injury, I had thought of possibly looking for work there after retirement. Well, I had my retirement now, much sooner than expected—and who knows what might lie ahead after completion of my healing.

In spite of the apparent bleakness of the moment, I really came to believe there might be something better and more important ahead. The dark night of the soul began to brighten just a bit.

CHAPTER SEVEN

Although the pain made each day an ordeal, there was progress on many fronts. My left leg was improving; I could now move all the muscles in the leg. Even my right leg was beginning to show some signs of life.

With this improvement, I was fitted for braces which covered both legs and reached to the waist. My first attempt to get into them was painful, exhausting, and ludicrous. After about thirty minutes, I made it, but I couldn't imagine going through this routine every day. I could make no movement whatever when I first stood up with the help of an aide. But at least I was standing; life looked so much different and better from this perspective.

One evening during dinner, I noticed there was a new face at one of the tables. His name was Tony. He was the thirteen-year-old boy who had survived the recent accidents which had killed both his parents and left him crippled. His spinal cord had been severed, and he would have to spend the rest of his life in a wheelchair. Immediately my heart went out to him.

I soon found out, however, that no sympathy should be wasted on Tony. He was happy, jovial, and a pleasure to be around. The center was never the same after his arrival. He loved humor and practical jokes as much as I did, and we soon became compatriots. Once after I had done some prank in which he was the recipient, I received my just reward when I tried to turn on my personal TV set that evening. All the knobs had been coated with butter. As I recoiled from the greasy mess, I saw some kind of motion at my door. I quickly pedaled my wheelchair to the hallway and saw a retreating wheelchair and the back of Tony's head as he rolled into his room. On another occasion, he took down a fire hose located on the wall near my room and dragged it in front of my door. I couldn't get up and over the hose while in my wheelchair, and I found the hose quite difficult to pick up and put back in place. What's more, he was continually trying to fabricate a romantic liaison between me and a particularly attractive, unmarried nurse.

I found in thirteen-year-old Tony the encouragement I needed to make the most of adversity. I also saw the transforming, positive effect he had on others and vowed to emulate his behavior. If he could laugh and enjoy life in spite of his shattering tragedies, then anyone could. He would serve as a model of inspiration for me through the trials which still lay ahead.

There was some positive change for me every day now. By the end of March, the doctors were talking about my going home for a weekend to see how I would fare. Tom Ballard promised to help, and he was given advice on what to do and not do. Luckily, because there was no cooking facility in his basement area, he had had access to my kitchen and was already used to cooking there. He also enjoyed it and agreed to take care of my meals for the time being.

All the news was not good, however. During routine x-rays, calcium stones were discovered in my bladder. I learned that catheters, upon which I still relied to void my kidneys, often cause these stones, and they would have to be removed. The special calcium-restricted diet, which had been the regimen since my birthday in Norton Hospital, had been aimed at reducing the chances of these stones forming. Now I knew why I couldn't have dairy products and other calcium foods. In the adjoining Jewish Hospital I had surgery to remove the stones. My therapy and muscle strengthening, however, took a recess for a few days.

Yet my recovery and progress continued to surprise the doctors and other medical experts. One of the younger doctors, who was interning at the rehab center, was especially conservative in his outlook for the future. I am sure he wanted to avoid the disappointment of unrealistic expectations, but he continually underestimated my progress. First, he doubted that I would regain much control over my left leg; then, after this began to occur, he was sure I wouldn't get any return in my right leg. When this happened, he cautioned me about the long-term problems of probable inadequate bladder and bowel control.

I went home for a weekend in early April. Tom and other friends helped transfer me in my wheelchair from the car into my home. As I was being lifted up the front steps of my apartment building, I saw Allibe, my cleaning lady for several years, on the porch of the house next door where she also worked. A couple of years earlier I had visited the local Methodist church where her husband was the minister. At the conclusion of one of his invigorating sermons, he announced that Allibe wanted to make some remarks. She got up and told the congregation how much she appreciated my visit and asked me to make some comments. Surprised at this invitation, I'm not sure what I said. Then to my discomfort, she began praising me, noting as proof of my saintliness the fact that I didn't smoke. She obviously was proud to introduce me to her congregation, and I was proud to be her friend, as well as her employer. We really did share a mutual feeling of respect and love for each other.

When I saw her on the porch next door, I waved, and she waved back and quickly disappeared. Much later she told me that she went back inside to hide her tears and wasn't sure she could continue to work for me because of her emotional response to my condition. She and her husband had had my parents over for dinner at their house during the bleak and early days of my recovery. At first, she had been relieved to learn that my assailants were not black, as though it might affect her employment or my friendship with her because she, too, was black. She was another of the wonderful and dear people who would be so helpful to me in the months and years ahead.

My dog, Vickie, met me at the car. At first, she seemed to have difficulty recognizing me or accepting the fact that I was still alive. But in a few minutes, it was obvious she remembered, and she wouldn't leave my side.

It was good to be home, but there were many adjustments to be made. My wheelchair was too wide to go everywhere, and I learned to change my routines in a hurry. The weekend passed quickly with many friends stopping by to greet me. I had been given an extra hour on Sunday evening before returning to the rehab center in order to attend my study group's meeting at my apartment. All in all, the weekend was a thrilling yet strenuous experience. I was glad to get back in my bed at the rehab center where I didn't feel like such a burden on others; at least, the people here were trained and being paid for attending to me.

I went home again in late April to stay for a month or so. Dr. Kelley wanted me to come back after that period for firsthand observation of my progress and for another attempt to get my kidneys voiding on their own. The doctors, as well as I, were beginning to be concerned whether I might have to rely on a catheter the rest of my life. Not only were there many, many inconveniences to this arrangement, but infection was a continual danger. One young man who had been in the same room with me for awhile had recently lost a kidney through infection.

As the time approached for me to go home on what was

to be essentially a permanent basis, I began to feel apprehensive. I couldn't believe I felt this way. Leaving a hospital environment and going home had been my fantasy and goal for months, and now I was uncomfortable with the thought of leaving the security of the rehab center and its trained staff. What would real life in a wheelchair be like? I could now slowly walk with the aid of my waist-high brace and with my crutches, but most of my time was spent in bed or in the wheelchair. The therapists instructed me to get out each day when I got home and walk as much as possible. They gave me directions on climbing and descending the four or five steps from my porch to the sidewalk.

The first few days at home were a real burden to Tom and other friends who helped. There was quite an adjustment for me. Although I would go out and walk the sidewalks of Belgravia Court once each day, most of the time, because of the pain, was spent lying down listening to music or watching television. I was alone through a large part of the day and really missed people, including the nurses and other medical people to whom I had become accustomed.

Vickie was present everywhere I went, however, and I never realized how great a bond could develop between human and animal. I had bought her as a puppy for fifteen dollars seven years before, but she began coughing when we got home. The veterinarian said she had distemper, so I took her back to the lady from whom I had purchased her. The lady said all I had to do was put Vicks® salve in her food. When that treatment worked, the name "Vickie" had been a natural selection.

She had been touted by her seller as a small rat terrier, but, as Vickie grew, it became obvious there was more involved than just a terrier. She matured into a medium-sized, extremely intelligent dog, whose parentage was probably rat terrier and German shepherd. She now seemed to have a sixth sense about my condition. Whenever a series of excruciating leg pains and spasms approached, Vickie would get up and come to wherever I was and lay her head as close to me as possible. Her obvious understanding and caring was very empathetic and comforting.

The phone rang one day; a policeman was calling. He said that the elder of my two assailants, the one who took the blame for shooting me, had pleaded guilty and been given twenty-one years' imprisonment. He had a previous conviction, had violated his probation from that conviction, and had been on a spree of armed robberies when my shooting occurred. He had been apprehended, not by the police, but by his wife who turned him in to his probation officer for assaulting her. Confession to robberies and my shooting followed. His accomplice, who had agreed to testify against him, had received a suspended sentence.

I was relieved that this person was now out of public circulation. Obviously he was a chronic offender. However, I felt more sympathy than vengeance for him. How did someone end up in such dire straits and circumstances? What a difficult future and karmic consequences must surely lie ahead for him!

Three days a week I went to the rehab center as an outpatient for physical therapy. At first, friends took me there, but Dr. Kelley had ordered hand controls for my pickup truck and, as soon as they were installed, I decided to drive on my own.

The first block or two of my driving was a thrill—actually a hazard!—but thereafter it was easy and a whole new dimension was opened. Now I could travel, get something to eat easily at drive-in restaurants, and start to enjoy life a little more normally. I also continued to see improvement in my walking ability, especially the use of my left leg.

Just as I was beginning to enjoy life a little, I returned to the rehab center for the scheduled checkup. My x-rays showed new bladder stones, which would require surgery again for removal. My hospital stay was thus extended for another week or so. Worst of all, attempts to get my bladder to function without a catheter were unsuccessful. On the brighter side, Dr. Kelley ordered my brace cut back to cover just the legs. Although I was wobbly at first, I could now freely move both legs at the hip, the weight of the braces was considerably less, and I could put them on much easier.

My roommate for this hospital stay was a man in his early thirties who had sustained a broken back and a severed spinal cord. His wife visited him frequently. One day after she had left, he told me he knew I wanted to go to bed with her and that he would kill me if I paid any more attention to her. I was flabbergasted. She was attractive, and I had tried to be friendly whenever she was present, but I definitely had no designs on her. I talked to the center psychiatrist about the incident, and he stated that this kind of reaction is not unusual. The possibility of not being able to perform marital sex relations again often makes a person suspicious of those who physically can. My excellent recovery was more than my roommate could handle, so his judgment and perceptions were clouded. I was discreetly moved to another room shortly thereafter.

When I was discharged in early June, another return to the hospital was scheduled for August. Dr. Kelley intimated that if I didn't get back the normal functioning of my bladder then, I would probably have to rely on a catheter the rest of my life.

By the time I returned to the hospital in early August, I was able to walk in a reasonably normal fashion with my left leg, although I still required the brace on that leg and, of course, the right one also. Back in the hospital, there was good news. X-rays showed that I didn't have bladder stones this time.

As I watched on television the historic last days of the Nixon administration, I began the battle of what I hoped would be my last days with a urinary catheter. The first efforts weren't promising. On the third or fourth day, David Talley, an aide and pre-med student, came into my room with a urinal in his hand and promised that he was going to see that I succeeded this time. Following his directions and after straining and trying for several minutes without success, I asked him to leave and let me try it on my own. I think I knew it was then or never, and I put every ounce of energy into the effort. I doubt that I ever tried harder to do something and wondered if I might not cause some kind of internal damage. But then a couple of liquid drops appeared.

At first I thought it had been an accident, but then I did it again. When David came back, I showed him the results. He looked around, believing I had gotten someone else to do the job. But the only other person in the room was totally dependent on a catheter and was asleep. He insisted that I perform in his presence, and I did a little.

He then grabbed the urinal and ran from the room. In a couple of minutes, I heard the voice of one of the nurses speaking through the intercom system in my room. "It's liquid gold, Glenn! Congratulations!" Then she switched the intercom so it would reach all the rooms and said: "Attention, everyone! Glenn can pee again!" I heard shouts and applause throughout the ward.

I wasn't the least bit sensitive to such public airing of what in most circumstances would be a very private matter. In this setting, everyone understood the importance of such an accomplishment. Those who had gone through the same experience could relate to my elation, but for those who hadn't, it offered hope. I found out later that the medical staff had already written off my situation as hopeless. When I called my parents and gave them the good news, Mother began crying. A hometown friend and nurse had told her it was virtually impossible to recover bladder control after such a long period of inactivity.

This victory assured me of a somewhat normal life. Even though urination was an unbelievably strenuous effort now, it would improve in the days and months ahead. I was so excited and elated, I could hardly appreciate the signifi- cance of the television news that evening announcing Nixon's resignation—the first time ever for a president of the United States.

I shared a large room with three other patients. None of them was over twenty-two years of age. Two had been in- jured while riding on motorcycles; one of them had been hit by a truck, and the other skidded on loose gravel while making a turn. The third young man had fallen from some scaffolding at a painting job. All three were worse off than I. Two had their spinal cords severed, and the other had re- covered his ability to walk but had permanent mental damage from a head injury. As I looked around me, I de- plored the anguish and tragic loss of normal life for these young persons who were just entering what should be their prime.

Dr. Kelley was outspoken in his contempt for motor- cycles. He claimed that nearly half of his patients, mostly young men, were cycle-accident victims. He was a one-man crusade against motorcycles and a staunch proponent for use of helmets.

I learned also that one of the greatest burdens is that which affects family and loved ones. The family of the young man with the head injuries had concluded there was no way they could cope with his care; commitment to an institu- tion seemed likely. One of my roommates experienced a broken engagement while I was there. His betrothed came by to return his ring and tell him she didn't want to spend the rest of her life with a handicapped person. This kind of withdrawal and abandonment by those whose commit- ment should be the most dedicated adds significant emotional grief to patients' physical pain. I was extremely grateful that my closest friend, Tom Ballard, was willing to help me through my period of rehabilitation and recovery at home.

My own good fortune continued. By mid-September, I was in control of all my bodily functions. In a regular therapy visit to the rehab center, my therapist had me remove my left leg brace and walk to the rear door of the building. I had done this before, but this time she opened the outside door and told me to go on to my truck and return home without the left brace. She said I didn't have to come back for further therapy until my right leg had recovered more. I felt as if I were walking on air as I headed for my truck.

A medical friend had recently told me, "You don't realize how important your body is, even the little, simple functions, until you lose them. Then they become the most important things in life." I could certainly realize the truth of his observation. I had been very lucky. Many of the friends I had acquired at the rehab center didn't go home in such relatively good condition. I wasn't confined to a wheelchair; I could live a reasonably normal life. As my car dreams had seemed to promise, I had recovered my walking ability.

I also was convinced, as I left the rehab center that September day in 1974, that it was simply a matter of time before I would be discarding the brace on my right leg and seeing the end of my continual, consuming, enervating leg pains. They were with me all the time and prevented me from enjoying life. There were times when spasms in my legs were so overpowering that I would just double up in convulsions of pain. These episodes happened with regular frequency, probably on an average of every fifteen minutes. I knew that my condition was often a depressant to others, so I tried to cover up the pain as much as possible. But there were times when I just could not do so.

I was sure, however, that my pain would soon go away. Then my long night would be over, and the serendipity would surely be awaiting me.

CHAPTER EIGHT

I sold the apartment building in which I had been shot. The simple reason for doing so was the limited space and narrow doorways which weren't designed for a wheelchair. I still relied on a wheelchair except when walking outside. As a long-term investment, Tom Ballard and I had purchased an old home about two years earlier a block away on St. James Court; the building was divided into four rental apartments. I now had some remodeling done to one of these apartments, and Tom and I moved there in the summer of 1974. The new quarters and my improved mobility made life there much easier.

St. James Court is an attractive, block-long area lined with trees and old Victorian homes. The centerpiece of the court is a three-tiered fountain. The court had in recent years, after a period of neglect, been renovated and become a popular residential neighborhood. Immediately behind my home was a large, imposing, stone church adorned with spires and a huge stained-glass window, all of which were works of art. It was a beautiful and graceful area in which to live.

One day while outside, I saw the minister of the church. He hadn't seen me since I had been shot and asked why I was walking with a leg brace and crutches. I told him. He was genuinely upset and critical of me for not carrying a gun for protection. I suggested that I probably couldn't have brought myself to shoot my attacker even if I had a gun. He couldn't understand my doubts and hesitancy about defending myself with lethal force.

As I thought later about that conversation, I wondered, too, at my reluctance to defend myself. Primarily, I found it difficult to consider actually killing another person. What had happened to me in recent years? I definitely recognized a change since my days in the air force when it had seemed an easy concept to kill rather than be killed. Luckily, I never had to do so, but defending the nation's interests with whatever force might be required was part of my military training and convictions.

The more I analyzed my feelings the more I realized the change had come from my involvement with the Edgar Cayce material. It stressed the value of human life and the consequences of taking another's life or doing evil to another person. Though someone with this attitude might lose his or her life, the soul would continue on, and the possible effect on the other side or in future earth lives would outweigh the inclination to take another life. For, in the words of the Bible, "whatsoever a man soweth, that shall he also reap." (Galatians 6:7) A Cayce reading added:

It is much better within the self mentally *and* physically that *ye* be the one mistreated than to mistreat someone else even in an inclination!   1183-3

Despite the above, the readings didn't condemn anyone for protecting his or her life or that of another nor in defending one's country or a rightful cause. During World War II, the Cayce readings did nothing to dissuade young men from going into the armed forces, which both of Cayce's sons did. Still, I preferred to err on the side of not killing someone wrongfully than being obsessed with saving my own skin. I marveled at how significantly, and yet subtly, my values and thinking had shifted since reading *The Sleeping Prophet* in 1968.

I noticed, too, a new empathy and regard for all forms of life. I had once enjoyed hunting as a sport. Now, while I didn't condemn anyone for doing so, I doubted that I could again kill rabbits or squirrels, much less larger game, for the simple sport or thrill of it. Maybe my closeness to Vickie had had something to do with this change. I truly felt more at one with all life and God's creations than I had just a few years before.

There were still long periods which I spent alone and often found myself reviewing the events of the past few months which had so turned my life around. Was I being punished for something I had done—if not in this lifetime, then possibly a past one? I had no idea, and the more I thought about it the more convinced I became that it really didn't matter. It seemed that the best way to handle my current situation in any event was to accept it as having some kind of meaning and purpose, try to make the best of the present circumstances while blaming no one, look for new opportunities, and keep my faith in God.

I read a lot of spiritual material, including the Bible, and I found particular inspiration in the book of Job. In a test of Job's faith, God had allowed a number of trials and tragedies to befall him. His faith in God prevailed, however, and Job ultimately received blessings in excess of those which he had lost. There was one particular question that Job asked which struck a responsive chord within me: "When I lie down, I say, When shall I arise, and the night be gone?" (Job 7:4) I frequently wondered and fantasized on when my night would be gone. When would I be healed and able to resume the important and normal incidents of life?

My study group continued to meet at my apartment and be a genuine support and inspiration to me. Around the end of August, one of the members, Lynn Weber, announced that her marriage was breaking up and that her husband, Bill, was leaving home. The group, as it had done for me, rallied to her support.

The next day Bill came by to visit. He said he had decided he just needed his freedom and, therefore, had to leave Lynn. Later, I would learn that he had actually fallen in love with a woman in Ohio. He asked that I, Tom Ballard, and the other members of the group help Lynn and her two boys during this period of adjustment. It was easy to make such a promise, and its fulfillment would change and enrich my life in the years ahead. Serendipity was still at work.

Shortly thereafter, Tom called Lynn, suggesting that he and I pick up some food and bring it by her place for dinner the following evening. We did so and enjoyed the visit with her and her two sons: Tom, who was then thirteen, and J.R., who was eleven. We had several such visits after that, and a very close friendship began to develop among all of us.

They lived in a residential area about fifteen miles from downtown Louisville, and it was obvious that a place closer to town would make getting a job and working easier for Lynn. She really did need employment now to support herself and the boys. Tom Ballard and I helped her look for a home in the old Louisville area where we lived.

After a few months, she obtained a job downtown, sold her home, and purchased a three-story, older residence about three blocks from where we lived. The house was large enough to allow the ground level to be separated and rented for additional income.

The most important result for me, however, was the company of Tom and J.R. after school hours and before Lynn came home. Often we all then had dinner together. They enjoyed card games, as did I, and my life, which had consisted of a lot of empty and lonely hours, took on new meaning and pleasure. I now had a family setting, with its attendant problems, but also its love and support. Everyone, I felt, benefited from the new arrangement.

For really the first time in my life, I also began to appreciate a genuine need for some kind of permanent, romantic relationship. As much as I cared for Lynn, she was more like a sister or family member and not a lover. Where could I, a not-so-young cripple, find the kind of woman I wanted? It was no longer easy nor desirable just "to play the field."

Here I was forty years old and had never been married. I contemplated the reasons for my bachelorhood. I definitely was interested in women and had always assumed I would get married someday. I had had a few serious relationships, but none of them had worked out. In most cases, this result had not really been my choice.

Maybe I would have married Lucille after college if the air force hadn't sent me immediately overseas for eighteen months of duty in Libya. I had thought I was in love with her, and we had communicated regularly after I left—that is, until her letter telling me she had decided to marry her former boyfriend and a law school friend of mine. There had been a couple of other "near misses," but always something unexpected seemed to intervene.

As a matter of fact, I think I had actually enjoyed my unmarried status. I liked the attention I received as a most-eligible bachelor. At the bank, at least half the employees, including those in the organizations under us, were women. At seminars and other meetings which they attended, I was a popular participant and could be sure of an invitation to be on the program. I even suspected that the mystique of being single may have helped me advance so rapidly in the bank hierarchy.

But certainly now conditions had changed. I remembered Martha, a woman in her twenties who worked for my Farm Credit Bank. She had on several occasions made her interest in me obvious, and she was certainly desirable. The more I thought of her, the more determined I became to seek her company. I called Martha, invited her to lunch, and then began seeing her fairly often. We genuinely seemed to enjoy each other, and I began to speculate what life might be like married to her. After waiting this long, however, I wasn't going to rush into anything too quickly. Then one day, she ended my speculation abruptly with a phone call canceling our next date and suggesting that we not see each other for a while. She claimed that being with me was too emotionally difficult. A few months later, I read in the bank newsletter that she and another bank employee were getting married.

In the next few years, there would be other similar, painful experiences.

Another Martha, whom I had known in high school, had lost her husband a few years before. She saw my mother one day and told her she had just broken an engagement with a man in Lexington and would love to hear from me. I had dated Martha during visits home from college and wasn't at all adverse to resuming this pursuit. I called her and wrote, and we made plans to visit. Before that meeting could take place, however, she wrote saying she had decided to go ahead and marry the man whose engagement she had broken.

I was fast learning to flow with circumstances, even when they didn't work out as I would have preferred and when they involved matters of the heart. As with so many other things in life, I felt that there must be a reason and purpose for my marital status—or lack of it. If this was the case, then there probably was something better in store for me. Serendipity was probably out there waiting for me to find and recognize it.

The Cayce psychic readings state in various ways that no one is in the circumstances or location he or she is by accident. Each situation has a purpose and meaning which we are challenged to build upon. That is part of the purpose of life: to learn to accept God's plan and make the most of it. It is the process of becoming a co-creator with the Almighty.

CHAPTER NINE

I returned to the rehabilitation center again in December of 1974 for a final checkup. I was doing well except for a pressure sore on my left foot. My sock probably had wrinkled and rubbed a sore on my heel when I walked. It had already existed for two or three weeks when the doctors first saw it. The wound was deep, and they were concerned. They wouldn't let me walk or wear a shoe for a week, but their treatments on the sore didn't result in any improvement. They began to wonder if it would ever heal because of poor circulation in the leg and because of my difficulty avoiding contact to that area. Thankfully, one of my favorite nurses—a large, always smiling, black woman—came to the rescue. She had heard of a gum powder used successfully in the Vietnam war to treat injuries that otherwise wouldn't heal. They tried it, and the results were phenomenal. I was healed in a week.

Life is dramatically changed and becomes precarious with paralysis. First, no feeling of external pain warns of impending danger. Then, one's normal control, balance, and strength are absent. Lying in bed or sitting in a wheelchair can present problems, especially in the form of pressure sores from being in one position too long. Special mattresses and sophisticated chair pillows are strongly advocated. It was a wholly different world in which I now existed. Falls and accidents were common, but by trial and error I had learned to fall with a minimum of damage. I also found it difficult to ask for help, but eventually learned that it is often necessary and usually not resented by others to do so.

I frequently took walks in nearby Central Park, where there were occasional falls. Once in the early days, I tumbled and couldn't get up. There was only one person in sight, and he was dressed in leather with a skull imprinted on his black jacket. His hair was long and unruly, and he wore a large, circular, dangling earring. I was frightened as I saw him make a beeline toward me. However, it was a good lesson in tolerance; he was extremely helpful and caring. He offered to assist me any time I needed help in walking, although I never ran into him again. On another occasion when I fell, a woman observed me getting up and said, "You don't know how much we appreciate what you did." Unless she was talking about the humorous entertainment my clumsiness provided, I assumed she thought I was a Vietnam veteran with battlefield injuries.

By the end of 1974, Dr. Kelley told me not to be surprised if the return of feeling in my still largely paralyzed right leg should cease. It was rare for such return to continue beyond a year, he warned.

His advice didn't concern me greatly. After all, I had been doing better than the doctors predicted ever since I was injured. I continued to exercise at home and expected my recovery to continue. It would be at least another year before I would concede that the return of feeling had ceased and recognize that my pain, which was still difficult to handle, might go on indefinitely. The worst part was when the always-present pain built up to such an extent that my muscles or nerves would go into spasms. This was still occurring about every fifteen minutes. On these occasions I would often double up with the pain, and everything around me would be blotted out of my senses, as I just tried to get through that period of overwhelming pain. It would usually last about a minute or so. For now, I had to believe that this kind of pain was temporary and would soon fade and be gone.

I still received disability benefits, and they were sufficient to take care of my expenses, but I wasn't satisfied just to remain disabled forever. Yet my pain was such that I couldn't seriously consider a regular job.

My study group asked me to represent them in the monthly A.R.E. Council meetings. The Council coordinated study group activity in the area. To make it easier for me, the Council agreed to meet in my apartment. It was the beginning of gradually working my way back into some kind of productive and social activity.

My interest in psychic and paranormal matters continued. In fact, it may have been heightened by my physical condition, which had now reached the limits of what conventional medicine could do. Maybe I could get some relief from psychic healers, whose ability I had heard about, but this was a phenomenon which I hadn't actually personally experienced or witnessed. I had read stories of healing, including many in the Bible. There were also various ministries on television in which healing seemed to be a successful mass production. One such healer, whom I had seen on television, came to Louisville for a service. Members of my study group, Marshall and June, urged me to attend, and they agreed to go with me.

There were at least 5,000 people present when the healer came on stage to the blare of music and spotlights. He began his healing program immediately. People in wheelchairs, crutches, and other evidences of affliction came forward to receive his healing commands and touch. Many appeared to be healed; some threw away crutches; others got out of their wheelchairs and shouted for joy as they walked away on their own. I was impressed, but I was positioned so far from the healer that I was hesitant to try to make my way through the crowd to reach him. Then he began walking around the auditorium. To my elation, he eventually headed up the aisle on which I was seated, healing people along the way with the command, "Be healed." Suddenly he stopped by me and put his hand on my head. My heart was beating in double time, and I said a prayer of thanksgiving. Instead of directing me to be healed, however, he simply said, "God be with you." I felt no change as he walked on.

Why hadn't I been healed when others apparently were? Why didn't he tell me to be healed? Did his statement, "God be with you," indicate a recognition that I was beyond healing? I left the service that day feeling worse mentally than when I had arrived. I wasn't sure exactly how to evaluate this particular healer. I suspected that, just as with psychics, some healers have significant talent; others, only minimal. Unfortunately, some purported healers probably have no talent at all. The whole area is one which invites fraud and charlatanism. Yet if there was any possibility of healing through this means, it was worth the effort. There was no other avenue open.

Clairvoyant psychics were another paranormal route that I felt I had to explore. I had seriously questioned whether or not it was proper to delve into psychic information. The test for me became one of checking accuracy over a period of time and ascertaining the information's apparent spirituality. Its spiritual quality was important to me because I felt that psychic talent could also be used malevolently. But determining whether or not something is spiritual is difficult and highly subjective. If psychic ability seemed spiritual and proved accurate, then it might be a gift from God as St. Paul had described in the New Testament. What's more, Jesus had said, " ... for the tree is known by his fruit" (Matthew 12:33), and the biblical fruits were those of the spirit: "love, joy, peace, long-suffering, gentleness, goodness, faith, meekness," self-control (Galatians 5:22-23). The psychic readings of Edgar Cayce had, for me, met this test; they reflected and called for these same spiritual characteristics.

I had often wished there were reliable living psychics available for information and guidance on difficult matters. For several years after discovering the Cayce material, I kept hearing the name Ray Stanford over and over again. Many people, including some of my friends, felt that the psychic information coming from him was excellent. I finally had joined his organization and had attended the first annual meeting of the Association for the Understanding of Man (A.U.M.) in Austin, Texas, in 1973, the summer before I was shot. With my recovery through traditional medical means now bogging down, I found myself frequently reflecting back to that trip.

One of the features of the three-day meeting in Austin had been a psychic reading by Ray for the entire group of 75 to 100 people. In the psychic session held at a local church, Ray spoke from an unconscious trance state. He warned the group about difficult times ahead, especially in the economic arena. At the time he said this, I wondered about the advisability of going ahead with my plans to build a recreational home on a lot I owned at Lake Cumberland. As if in response to my question, Ray then cautioned against anyone building recreational or second homes. I was impressed and took his advice. In view of the way things had turned out, I was extremely glad that I had.

Stanford also talked about Comet Kahoutek, which was scheduled to rendezvous with the earth in early 1974. The comet was to signal a period of extreme testing for the earth and that would especially be so, he said, for those who were assembled to hear these psychic comments. It would constitute a personal chastening which, in the long run, would help these individuals prepare for the spiritual trials which lay ahead during the latter part of this century.

This information had been on my mind often throughout the ordeal of my injury and recovery. It had seemed particularly relevant when I observed that my injury occurred on January 8, the day Comet Kahoutek was closest to the earth. It was also during this period and shortly thereafter that our economy fell apart as a result of the oil and gas shortages of the Arab embargo. All in all, I was quite impressed by Ray's predictions and the subsequent happening and timing of events.

I hadn't forgotten either the personal letter I received from Ray while in the hospital. He got word of my injury from Tom Ballard, who called the A.U.M. requesting prayers during the critical period of my hospitalization. Ray told me in the letter that he foresaw my recovery and a future visit to the A.U.M. in Austin. His prediction certainly buoyed my hopes at a time when events generally were quite bleak.

So I felt I had found at least two psychics whose ability seemed genuine. One was living; the other dead. I wasn't sure, however, how to evaluate psychic healers nor how to discern who among the many might be helpful for me.

But as friends recommended various healers, I welcomed the information and made a reasonable attempt to try them all. None of their efforts, however, met with any success. Sometimes their recommendations were rather bizarre.

One New Age doctor told my father I needed to eat a certain kind of soil and sent a small (although it looked awfully large to me) package of dirt. I never did get it down.

One of my study group friends had some obvious psychic ability of his own and came up with a remedy which he said had been given to him in a dream or vision. If I would take a cloth doll, which he supplied, and sew a "Jacob's ladder" stitch up the middle of the doll's back, I would be healed. At first I refused, but everyone seemed to think I should give it a try and maintain a good, cooperative attitude, so I did the stitching. Nothing happened.

Carl wasn't fazed, however. About a year later, he came to the group meeting and handed me a brown sack, tied with a nice red bow. He told me to open the sack after the group had left, which I did. It contained pieces of broken pottery. He called the next day with instructions. I could be healed if I would fit the pieces together, glue them, and thus reconstruct the flower pot. There were hundreds of small broken pieces. I refused. A couple of weeks later, I relented. It was important to Carl, and I knew his intentions were good. They were better than the results I derived from assembling the broken pot which I glued together over the next three days.

There were many others, and when the healers didn't succeed, I noticed a pattern among some of them. They rationalized the failure by indicating that I was blocking the healing or had insufficient faith for its success. But some didn't appear to be so egotistical. They evidenced genuine concern for my condition and seemed to be vessels of God's healing power.

The one who impressed me the most was Olga Worrall of Baltimore, Maryland. I had read a book about the healing ministry of her and her late husband, Ambrose. I learned that she had a healing session on Thursdays at her church in Baltimore and decided to go. The church was in a scenic setting near a rushing creek in a wooded residential valley. The service began in the early afternoon, and at the proper time I made my way to the front of the auditorium to receive her healing touch. When it came my turn, she placed her hand on my head and said a prayer. I felt powerful heat emanating from her touch. My pain and paralysis, however, didn't improve. Yet I remained hopeful and refused to deny the efficacy or potential of this unorthodox approach and my pursuit of it.

CHAPTER TEN

In February of 1976, Tom Ballard invited me to accompany him and his mother on an auto trip to visit his sister in Tucson, Arizona. His mother was going to stay in Tucson for a while, and Tom wanted company, particularly on the return journey. I decided to try the trip and made it in reasonably good condition. The only real problem I had was the pain, and by changing positions in the car, including lying down occasionally in the back seat, I did almost as well as I would have at home.

On the return east, we went by way of Austin, Texas. We visited Ray Stanford and his organization, the A.U.M. A small staff worked with Ray, and they were very friendly and accommodating. They invited us to go to lunch with them at a local health restaurant. I got to visit with Ray for quite some time, and he said my visit was just as he had visualized it some two years before. He told me about a book he had just finished on UFOs, which, he said, would "blow the lid off" government secrecy on and cover-up of the subject. Ray also predicted I would eventually be totally healed. My optimism and outlook were extremely positive when we left.

Later the same year, Tom, Lynn, her boys, and I took a two-week tour of the West. While it wasn't my first trip there—I had spent a year-and-a-half in California on air force duty in the early sixties—it was good to see again some of the beautiful spots of the West. Lynn and the boys had never been there, so their reaction and appreciation of the sights made mine even more enjoyable. I survived the trip reasonably well by spending most of the traveling time lying across the bunk in the top of Tom's pickup camper. J.R. and Tom Weber traveled in the camper with me.

The success of this trip prompted another one through the Northwest and Canada the following year. It even included an overnight ferry ride through the Inside Passage from Vancouver Island to Prince Rupert, British Columbia. That area plus the Canadian Rockies constituted the most scenic journey I had ever undertaken. I felt it exceeded the beauty of the Swiss Alps.

But it was a trip which I took earlier in 1977 that would ultimately have the greatest impact on my life. Martha Binford, the Kentucky A.R.E. Regional Representative, persuaded me to accompany her to the A.R.E. Congress in June at Virginia Beach, Virginia. It was my first visit there, and yet I immediately felt at home and met some of the most spiritually beautiful people I had ever encountered.

I had been concerned about my ability to get around at meetings and to cope with the pain. Walking with canes and a brace on my right leg allowed only limited mobility at any one time. I suffered some but made it without major problems. Everyone made a special effort to help me.

A.R.E. Congress is an annual event dating back to the days when Edgar Cayce was alive and would give a psychic reading for this group of his most ardent followers. Each year it draws many of those persons active in the organization's field work; a lot of "old-timers" make an effort to attend this once-a-year gathering. There are inspirational speakers as well as sharing by participants of their activities both at Virginia Beach and out "in the field." In many ways, Congress resembles a for-profit organization's annual stockholders meeting.

I was thrilled to get to meet authors and people about whom I had only read. They included Edgar Cayce's son and A.R.E. president, Hugh Lynn Cayce, Gladys Davis Turner (Edgar Cayce's secretary who recorded and typed the readings), Elsie Sechrist (author, lecturer, and study group promoter), Eula Allen (author and friend of Edgar's), and Mae St. Clair (close friend of the Cayce household who had assisted the work through the years). I heard firsthand stories about Edgar Cayce, the man, and of his unique talent which helped thousands. To be at the A.R.E. headquarters with these people was a dream come true.

I also regained some personal esteem which had disappeared in the long months of my rehabilitation and social isolation. Each year Congress officers are chosen to organize and lead the next year's meeting. At that time, selections were made by nomination and election. Dawn Ahart, of Los Angeles, was elected chairperson for the 1978 Congress. To my surprise and mild concern, I was elected vice chairperson.

During that week I was told that Hugh Lynn Cayce's son, Charles Thomas, wanted to see me. We finally saw each other in the parking lot on the last day of Congress. "I wonder if you would like to work at the A.R.E.," he began.

"I would love to if my health were better," I quickly responded.

We talked some more, and he asked me if I would keep such an option in mind and let him know if and when I ever felt ready to work at the A.R.E.

Almost as an afterthought, he asked, "Well, how about serving on the Finance Committee?" He explained that the committee met four times a year and made recommendations to the Board of Trustees about the organization's monetary decisions.

"We need someone with a legal and financial background who is drawing disability income so we don't have to pay him for his services," he jokingly added.

I quickly accepted this offer.

These developments operated as a healthy stimulant to my spiritual and emotional well-being. I would have plenty of time for the round-trip drive between Louisville and Virginia Beach four times during the coming year, and there was now some purposeful meaning and work to occupy my time.

At the September meeting of the Finance Committee, Charles Thomas told me there was a Japanese acupuncturist visiting the A.R.E. and that he wanted me to have a treatment. It was arranged for Saturday afternoon in the headquarters building—what fifty years earlier had been the Cayce Hospital. The Japanese doctor suggested that he could best work with me on the carpeted floor in one of the offices which was deserted on the weekend. For the treatment, he had me take off all my clothes and my leg brace. As I lay there totally naked on the floor, the doctor began inserting and twirling needles all over my body. When he got to the paralyzed areas, mostly my right leg, he mumbled something in Japanese and then explained in English, "Bad, bad!" Of course, I already knew that much. Finally, he concluded the treatment by putting a piece of a cork-like substance on the end of each big toe and setting them on fire.

As I lay there nude with smoke curling up from each big toe, I heard the door open—and then close quickly. Shortly thereafter, it opened and closed again.

Some time after the unsuccessful acupuncture treatment, Charles Thomas told me he had been working in his office nearby and heard a gasp. He came out and saw a woman shutting the door to the office where I was and then fleeing down the hall. He then came and opened the door and saw me lying on the floor naked with smoking toes. He said he never saw the lady again and wondered with amusement what she had reported to others about the weird and strange events at the Cayce place.

The next year—1978—was even more significant for me.

In June, I attended Congress again, and Dawn Ahart did such an excellent job as Congress chairperson that my position as vice chairperson was largely ceremonial, which suited me just fine. During Congress, I was notified that I had been elected to the A.R.E. Board of Trustees; it met on the weekend right after the four annual Finance Committee meetings. My duties and involvement with the A.R.E. were continuing to expand, and I was pleased.

Late that summer back in Louisville, the local A.R.E. Council was considering a retreat for local members. Each year we usually went to a nearby park for a weekend retreat, but I suggested that that year we go to the Lake Cumberland area. It was about a three-hour drive and would be more expensive. A Council majority finally approved my recommendation. About twenty-five people made the trip.

I took my boat and gave everyone a brief ride on the lake. We managed to intersperse a few talks on spiritual matters and meditation sessions into the festivities. On Sunday, I pursuaded everyone to go with me on a hike. I think there were a few reservations about such strenuous activity, but no one wanted to raise the issue or be outdone by a cripple relying on canes to get around. We drove to the Yahoo Falls parking area.

The hike was only about a mile, but there was a long flight of stairs to descend, then a difficult return climb. Yet I was determined to make it. Eventually we all arrived at a small footbridge just downstream from the falls. From the bridge, there was a great view of Yahoo Falls. I was ready to stop and suggested that we meditate in this magical spot. For me, the meditation was emotional and extremely powerful. During this quiet time, I recalled those days in General Hospital when I had been so hungry and thirsty and fantasized about being right here. I had finally made it and brought with me the special friends of the study group and council.

I told the others of the significance and meaning of this event. They rejoiced with me, and we all made the climb back to our cars without major problems. I was delighted finally to have made this journey with this group.

Tom Ballard, the Webers, and I took another trip to the West in July, covering the American Southwest and Baja California in Mexico. Returning through Utah, we had scheduled a rafting trip on the Colorado River. The evening before it was to begin, in a motel room in Moab, I slipped on the wet linoleum in the bathroom. Having just taken a bath, I didn't have on my right leg brace. I fell on the leg. It popped, but seemed to be O.K.

In the night, I woke up and could hardly breathe, but assumed it was the altitude and finally went back to sleep. In the morning, I felt awful but was determined to do the rafting. During the six-hour float through the rapids and majestic scenery, I was miserable. When we left the raft and started up a slight slope to the waiting bus, I went part of the way and could go no farther. Tom and the Webers virtually carried me to the bus. I was sick and couldn't breathe. By the time the bus arrived back in Moab, I was feeling somewhat better and was ready for the three-hour ride to Ouray, Colorado, where we had reservations for the night.

Tom and Lynn insisted that I see a doctor, and after much argument we went to the emergency room of the local hospital. The doctor who saw me concluded I had picked up an infection and gave me a prescription to fight it. Unfortunately, that day was a Mormon religious holiday, and the drugstores were closed.

We made it to Ouray, and I purchased and began taking the prescribed medicine the next day. The doctor had said it would take two or three days for the medicine to have an effect, so we kept to our planned itinerary, although I didn't feel any better.

The following day was spent on a narrow-guage train ride from Durango to Silverton, Colorado. It was the high point of our trip, but I couldn't enjoy it. That evening we drove sixty miles to Pagosa Springs, where we were scheduled to stay. Lynn and Tom called a local doctor and described my condition; he volunteered to meet me in his office. They finally persuaded me to go.

After various examinations and tests, the doctor gravely gave his advice. He thought I had experienced a stroke or heart attack and that my life was in serious jeopardy if I continued traveling on to Kentucky. He had already ordered an ambulance to take me back to Durango, which had a hospital with facilities sufficient to take care of a case as serious as mine. I argued and argued, but finally his severity and evident concern for my condition caused me to relent. I will never forget that sixty-five-mile night ride with flashing red lights through the mountains of Colorado. Lynn and Tom followed us and stayed with me until I was checked into a bed in the Intensive Care Unit. It seemed like déjà vu from a few years before.

It was late the next day before a final diagnosis was made. I had cracked the tibia in my right leg when I fell in the motel. Part of the body's fight against such injury is to send lymphocytes through the bloodstream. They had lodged in my lungs and caused nausea and an inability to breathe. My lack of feeling in the leg had hidden from me the nature and fact of the injury.

There was general relief with this diagnosis, but the break required me to stay off the leg for a time, and I couldn't continue the journey home. Lynn and the boys drove the truck and camper back; Tom Ballard stayed with me. He ended up calling a friend to fly out to Durango for a few days, and they spent part of the time touring the area with an extended vacation in a very scenic part of the United States. Their presence and company during my hospital stay was most welcome and helpful.

After eight or ten days, the doctor decided I could fly home if I kept on my leg brace (which gave the fracture some support) and stayed off the leg as much as possible. Home looked unusually good when I finally arrived there on an August evening in 1978. For several weeks, I spent most of my waking hours back in the wheelchair from which I thought I had graduated.

My travels for the year weren't over, however. I had the Board trip to Virginia Beach in late September as usual, but a trip to Wisconsin in November was scheduled rather spontaneously.

At the September A.R.E. Board meeting, Charles Thomas Cayce told me of a doctor friend who was experimenting with and using both conventional and nonconventional methods for treating pain. The doctor was Norman Shealy, and he operated a clinic in La Crosse, Wisconsin. I decided to write the clinic, and the next thing I knew I was scheduled for a two-week session in the early part of November.

I learned much from the trip and found the people there to be as dedicated and service-oriented as those at the A.R.E. in Virginia Beach. I hadn't known what to expect but was pleased from the start at the pastoral setting in which the clinic was located. Actually, it was located in a large house where the Shealy family resided. They had a dining area on the first floor and a meeting room in the basement large enough to accommodate the thirty persons of our session. The program lasted two weeks and involved treatment with acupuncture, electrical stimulation, biofeedback, meditation, musical relaxation, and even psychic healers. Much of the treatment was psychological, with an apparent recognition that mind can do much to heal, and, conversely, that negative thoughts can bring on pain and illness. Considerable attention was given to teaching us how to observe the body and come to love it. I was surprised to learn how frequently disease is brought on by religious and societal condemnation of the body as an instrument of sin and evil desire. Dr. Shealy and his staff taught us that the desires of the body are to be honored and used as a holy expression of creativity. Much of his teaching and treatment sounded like the Edgar Cayce readings put into practical application.

Dr. Shealy was a very interesting person. He was cockily sure of himself and had pioneered some very important advances in medical treatment, including modalities that were aspects of the newly emerging "holistic healing." He was a genius with the usual idiosyncracies that go with such talent. I was particularly amused at his unequivocal stand against tobacco and smoking. He allowed no one to light a cigarette near the premises. I heard a story from one of his staff members about the time he found a cigarette butt floating in one of the bathroom toilets. He ordered everyone out of the house and began a search of each person for cigarettes. Apparently none were found, and his interrogations produced negative results as well. The whole day's agenda had been disrupted in an effort to determine who had broken the smoking ban.

I personally liked Dr. Shealy, and he spent a lot of time with me trying to find something that would reduce my pain. One of the treatments was a three-day trial of D-Phenyalanine. On the second morning of taking the tablets, I felt unusually good. There was virtually no pain all morning long, and I told everyone of my good fortune. As I gave a report to Dr. Shealy, there were tears of joy in my eyes. He, too, was emotional as he told me he had feared that nothing could be done for my particular kind of pain. Gradually in the afternoon, however, the pain returned. Before I left, they tried the regimen again, but there was no response this time. But all around me were people getting relief in their fight against pain. I came away with a healthy respect for unconventional and holistic approaches to medicine.

On Friday, our last scheduled day at the clinic, word was received of a snowstorm expected later in the day. I left around noon and barely escaped its brunt. The roads were getting slick, but not impassable, as I headed south.

A series of cobra venom injections had been prescribed by Dr. Shealy for me when I returned home. It involved a month-long cycle of shots, which had been successful with others in reducing some kinds of pain. I faithfully performed the regimen back in Louisville, but it failed to alleviate my chronic pain.

I was, nevertheless, determined to keep trying. I refused to give up hope. It wasn't bravery, just the only acceptable alternative I had.

In addition to mainstream medicine, I continued to explore nontraditional approaches. Dr. Shealy had strongly recommended a psychic in Baltimore who was also a medical doctor. So, on my next trip to Virginia Beach, in January 1979, I went by way of Baltimore for a psychic diagnosis by Dr. Robert Leichtman.

Dr. Leichtman lived in a nice but not ostentatious home and neighborhood. He was very pleasant and interested in the welfare of the A.R.E. I found out later that he had written a book about information supposedly channeled from Edgar Cayce on the other side. After a few minutes, he laid back in his chair and went into a light trance. He then indicated he was ready for me to ask questions. I had my tape recorder ready to capture his answers. I asked him about my physical condition and whether I could be healed.

In a slightly altered voice, he said my spinal injury had caused considerable shock and trauma to the spinal cord. He "saw" pieces of bone fragments still near the injury site. (Years later this fact would be confirmed through Magnetic Resonance Imaging or MRI.) He indicated that I could be healed but that scar tissue was a major block and would have to be overcome. He claimed that the technique for combating the effects of scar tissue wasn't now available but would be known and used in the future.

"I see you getting a little better each year with what appears to be total healing, or nearly so, somewhere down the road. You will be quite active in your seventies and eighties."

Near the end of the reading, he claimed that a doctor or someone from Texas would play a role in my healing. But other than my keeping a good diet and visualizing a sound and healthy spinal cord and nerves, he had no specific recommendations for treatment.

After coming out of trance, Dr. Leichtman related what he had "seen" to what he knew as a medical doctor. He indicated scar tissue is a difficult condition to treat and noted that much research was being done on the subject. (In subsequent years, medical investigators determined that scar tissue is a major deterrent to nerve and central nervous system tissue regrowth, although this fact wasn't generally recognized at the time of my reading from Dr. Leichtman.)

I paid him a modest fee for his services and headed to Virginia Beach. I didn't have any new information or advice to work with, but his comments certainly held promise and hope for the future. Most people deteriorate a little each year; he claimed I would be a little better physically with each passing year. If true, it would be a novel way to counteract aging.

Toward the close of 1978, I received a letter from Charles Thomas Cayce asking me to consider a job opening at the A.R.E. I replied that I still didn't feel ready nor, in this case, qualified. The position was accounting and finance related, and my bank experience really didn't give me that kind of specialized expertise. Twice now I had turned down opportunities to work at the A.R.E.

Was I overlooking serendipity? Was God opening a door which I should enter?

I made a personal vow. If God wanted me to work at the A.R.E. in my present condition, then another job would have to open up. I promised myself that if another were offered and I was halfway qualified, I wouldn't turn it down.

CHAPTER ELEVEN

The next two years passed rather routinely. I purchased a twelve-unit apartment building, which required some renovation but was in reasonably good condition and seemed to be a sound investment for me. I would have no retirement benefits ahead and needed to plan for some kind of future income.

I put two of the ground-floor apartments together into one unit, and Tom Ballard and I moved into it. We sold the building he and I owned on St. James Court. Within another year, he bought a building of his own and moved into it.

I had depended greatly on Tom. I don't know how I could have made it in the years after my injury without his help and the sharing of expenses. Yet I think we both realized, without any rancor between us, that it was time to go our separate ways. He no longer participated in the study group activity, which continued to be so important and helpful to me. We had different interests, and I could now get along on my own. A friend I had known years before in Owensboro, Kentucky, had recently moved to town and was looking for an apartment. The need for someone to share my large apartment had thus been easily solved, and I continued to have the Webers as the family support which was so necessary for me.

At the January 1981 A.R.E. Board of Trustees meeting,

Charles Thomas Cayce asked me if I would consider taking the newly created position of Director of Development. The third call had come, but was I qualified for the job? It consisted mainly of fund-raising for the organization—a thankless task in my eyes. I had no experience in fund-raising, but then I learned that a large part of the job's duties consisted of working with estates, personal wills, and other forms of specialized giving. My legal background would undoubtedly come in handy here.

Presently I was financially secure with insurance and Social Security disability payments, and I would lose them both if I took the A.R.E. position. Could I handle a full-time job? What would I do if I couldn't? But somehow I knew I would never feel right about myself if I didn't make the move and try. If it turned out I was physically unable to make the grade, surely some other gate would open. The Cayce philosophy had convinced me that I should flow with opportunities as they presented themselves and that, if I did, God would take care of me. I needed to have faith, and serendipity might also be out there waiting to be claimed. Instead of security, maybe there was a greater treasure to be had.

I promised Charles Thomas and the Board that if no one else worked out for the position, I would take it after a period of time to complete personal matters in Kentucky. Another Trustee, Elsie Sechrist, asked me how long I needed. I told them a year; surely the job would be better filled by someone else by then. At least I had fulfilled my personal vow; I had accepted the next A.R.E. offer, however provisionally. If I did end up taking the job, I thought that surely Vickie, who was now approaching sixteen years of age, would no longer be around. I knew she was too old to make such a major move, and I couldn't stand the thought of deserting her at an age not many dogs attain. I also needed time to adjust to such a radical change in my life style from security without working to depending upon satisfactory work performance for a living.

My physical condition was the main question mark in considering the A.R.E. job. I could get around reasonably well with the aid of the right leg brace and a cane, but the pain continued to interfere with my mental concentration and energy levels. I discussed these issues with Charles Thomas Cayce, and he assured me they would help me work around the obstacles.

At one point, it looked as if someone else was going to be hired as Development Director, but the appointment fell through. In September, I formally accepted the job and promised to move to Virginia Beach in the spring.

Making such a move by myself seemed physically impossible, but "the forces" apparently were working in my behalf again.

About a year before, a young man had attended our study group for a time, and we had become good friends. Gary Rose was a product of a broken home who had been forced to leave his mother's household and provide for his own support at the tender age of fifteen. Now, nearly twenty, he was employed at the local school for the blind and was on an intense spiritual search of his own. He felt socially uncomfortable with the group but was very interested in the Edgar Cayce psychic material. He and I began having dinner together about once a week, and we both enjoyed our stimulating conversations about the nature of life and God.

We were drawn even closer by a research and writing project. Years before, in reading *Edgar Cayce's Story of Jesus* by Jeffrey Furst, I had been particularly impressed with how the Cayce readings supported the Bible's story of Jesus and also weaved additional information into the narrative. I was unsure, however, about the statements by Cayce that the soul of Jesus had lived thirty lifetimes before attaining the perfect and sinless one as Jesus. This concept didn't seem to fit with my conventional religious upbringing, which said that Jesus was the Son of God who presumably came to earth for the first time as Jesus. Eventually I became intrigued with the past-life idea and began a lengthy search for any kind of historical support for the earlier lives of Jesus.

At some point, I got Gary interested in the Jesus past-life research, and he was very helpful in assisting me to get around and look for ancient Christian and Jewish documents that might bear on the question of whether Jesus had incarnated earlier. It was also good just to have someone from whom I could bounce ideas and add inspiration to the seemingly impossible task of finding information on this elusive subject. We made journeys to libraries as far distant as Philadelphia. As the research grew, I began to contemplate the possibility of putting the material into a book.

One day in the fall of 1981, after having made my decision to move to Virginia Beach, Gary was complaining about his work at the school for the blind and an incident that had seriously troubled him. I asked if he would like to move to Virginia Beach. A few weeks later, he announced that he *did* want to go. His decision brought considerable relief to me. Because of my physical limitations, I had been concerned about moving, finding a place to live, and adjusting to a new environment on my own. Now I would have some help and support.

Meanwhile, I continued to stay alert for any source of information that might aid my healing. From my A.R.E. friends, I kept hearing about a psychic in Florida named Al Miner. Every report was positive. I decided to get a psychic reading from him. Maybe I could get some clues on how to treat my lingering paralysis and pain. Or perhaps I could find out why I was injured, what were some of my past lives, and whether it was wise for me to have accepted the A.R.E. position as Director of Development.

It took several months to get the psychic reading, but it

was received before I left for Virginia Beach and was quite powerful. Every time I read it, I got new insight and inspiration. There was suggested treatment for my physical condition, and the reason for my injury was also given. It said the purpose was to get me moving in a more meaningful direction and to let my experiences serve as an example for others. I could write or talk about them to various audiences. The past-life information was also helpful. I supposedly had had a past life with Gary in which he had saved my life and introduced me to a new and better spiritual philosophy. I was being given the opportunity to help him in this lifetime. I was also encouraged to take the A.R.E. position.

Maybe the most important information I received through Al Miner was from a follow-up reading in the summer of 1982 (see Appendix A). It presented past-life information which had relevance to my research on the possible previous lives of Jesus. I reputedly had been part of the Council of Nicaea, where the issue was raised of whether Jesus was a human soul who worked His way to Godhood or God who became human for a time. The claim of past lives for Jesus was implied in the minority view of the Council delegates who said that Jesus was a soul who had worked His way to Godhood. The reading said I was banished from the Council for my support of this minority view and eventually lost my life over it. What's more, I was back now to raise the issue again and, according to the reading, this viewpoint was in fact correct.

I had been worried for some time that a biblical scholar or equivalent should be doing the Jesus past-life research instead of me, but I hadn't asked Al Miner the specific question of whether it was proper for me to be working on such a controversial subject. For that matter, I hadn't asked *anything* on the subject. Nonetheless, the reading provided personal past-life information intimating it was exactly what I should be involved in now.

I did some research into the Council of Nicaea and found that one of the delegates had actually been named Maris, the name given for me in the psychic reading. He was bishop of Chalcedon, a city on the outskirts of present-day Istanbul, Turkey, and he had sided with the dissident Nicaean minority. I then remembered the strong past-life feelings I had experienced when I toured the old Byzantine Christian churches near Istanbul during my stint in the air force.

My encounters with psychic information didn't end with Al Miner. Gary had become somewhat interested in the spiritualist movement and asked me early in 1982 if I would like to go with him to Tampa, Florida, for an international spiritualist meeting. I knew that as soon as I had a full-time job, I probably wouldn't be able to take some time off, so I agreed to go. The meeting was in February at a major motel near the Tampa airport. Some of the best spirit mediums in the world were present, and it turned out to be an eye-opening experience. I saw appearances and heard voices of "spirits" under conditions which to my critical eye seemed impossible to have been the product of fraud or fakery.

The first afternoon about fifty of us assembled in a small room with a medium present. We watched as he entered a small, curtained cubicle. After a short period of attunement, his changed voice began giving messages from the "other side" to those of us present. I doubted if Gary or I would receive any such word; no one there really knew us.

To my surprise, Gary was told something from a deceased relative. It seemed to have meaning for him. I was still doubtful about my name being called, however.

Suddenly a familiar voice said, "Edward Glenn, this is your Aunt Mary."

My mother's older sister, Mary Edna, had died a year or so before. To my knowledge, no one there knew anything about her or that my first name is Edward. I never used my first name, but Aunt Mary often had. After all, the "Edward" had been given to me from the name "Edna," in her honor.

She continued on: "I am doing fine and want you to know I love you."

She said one or two other things, but it was her final comment that struck home:

"Just do the best you can, honey child."

"Honey child" was a term only she used for me, and she had done so on many occasions. No one there or virtually anywhere could have known this. Surely I really had been in touch with my Aunt Mary!

There was an even more spectacular event the next afternoon. Fifty or sixty of our group assembled in a room with no windows and only one door. Each person was carefully searched as he or she entered the room. When everyone was present, the door was shut and sealed with heavy brown paper taped over the doorway. Motel personnel then sealed the door from the other side. Again, a medium entered the curtained cubicle at the front of the room. The lights were turned off in anticipation for what was hoped to be visitations by spirits who would use ectoplasm from the medium's body to appear before us.

At first nothing happened, but then an eerie, luminous form began to take shape across the room. It moved slightly, then stopped in front of one of our members. We were all sitting around the room with our chairs against the walls. A message was given to the person before whom the "spirit" had stopped. Then the form vanished. This kind of phenomenon was repeated in a number of instances, although sometimes only a voice would be heard from a spirit guide. When there was an actual spirit appearance, each was in a different form and countenance. Some presented material gifts to the person they were visiting. I received some advice, which I have since forgotten, from an American Indian guide, who didn't appear in visible form.

At one point, a luminous form appeared in front of the lady sitting next to me on my left, who was from Germany.

In a firm voice the form identified itself as St. Germaine. He praised the lady for the work she was doing in Germany. Almost imperceptibly a jeweled sword appeared in the "spirit's" hand. He knighted the lady with it and left it in her possession, as he slowly faded from view. He had had distinctive facial features, which I could make out and which, to me, seemed appropriate for St. Germaine.

The session concluded a short time thereafter, and the lights were turned on. The taped seals over the door had remained unbroken. The medium slowly came out of his cubicle, a little groggy and dazed but otherwise unchanged. I looked at the sword in the lap of the lady next to me. It was beautiful and quite large. I touched it, and it was genuine metal. To my logical mind, it was impossible for anyone to have smuggled it into the room as well as some of the other items that had materialized before us. I didn't understand the strange things I had seen and heard.

On the last evening, about one hundred people attended a special event called cardwriting. A stack of blank three-by-five-inch index cards were shown to us, and we were invited up to examine them personally to verify that they had nothing written on them. Next they were dropped into an empty bucket on a table. The bucket, too, had clearly been shown to contain nothing. The leader then dropped a number of short, sharpened pencils into the bucket and covered it with towels and a blanket. He asked about a half dozen of the best psychic mediums present to come forward and hold the bucket aloft. Soon the bucket was moving around in unbelievable gyrations, at one point so briskly that the holders could barely maintain their grasp. None of the hands could reach into the bucket with its elaborate wrapping and, even without it, we would have seen the effort if anyone had tried. After about fifteen minutes of this activity, which I initially supposed was the entire show, the bucket was placed back on the table and unwrapped. The leader then reached in, retrieved the cards, and one by one called out the names on them.

To my mild surprise, my name was called, and I went forward and claimed my card. Near my name was a penciled message from a Dr. Lincoln, whom I had been told earlier was one of my spirit guides. It said, "If one door closes, another will be open." I read the message of serendipity into this comment.

Immediately after the distribution of cards, the program took a stretch break. As I got up to walk around, I laid the card on my chair. I noticed for the first time that there was something also written on its back side. When I picked up the card, I was awestruck as I read the message: "Edgar Casey. I Help with the Book." No one there other than Gary—who was as shocked as I and had talked to no one about the project—knew that I was working on a book involving information from the Edgar Cayce readings. Although the name Cayce was misspelled, I had to conclude that this was some kind of legitimate message phonetically received from the other side. If someone had gone to this much trouble to concoct a fraud, they surely wouldn't have messed up on the spelling. I decided I was just going to have to take the incident on faith, and it reinforced my resolve to put the results of the Jesus past-life research into book form.

My experiences with spiritualism had been truly remarkable. I had a very healthy respect for the psychic information I had received. It had been helpful to me. Although I found something lacking insofar as it becoming my church and primary source of spiritual guidance and inspiration, there had been other benefits. There was great value, I felt, in the evidence of the continuity of life which came from spiritualist contact with entities from the other

side. My faith in a person's survival of death had been reinforced, and these paranormal events had helped confirm
other beliefs which were based upon the concept of the
human soul's indestructibility.

After I returned home, I received a call from someone in
California named Brad. He apologized for calling and for
the unusual reasons for doing so. He explained that his purpose was related to his recent psychic reading from Al
Miner. In describing Brad's past life in Greece, the reading
stated that he should contact Glenn, who was a brother of
his in that life. Later, Al had supplied him with my full name
and phone number. We both enjoyed talking about this possible connection in a foreign land generations ago, and he
said he would have called earlier but was at a symposium in
Phoenix, Arizona. I asked him what kind of symposium it
was, already suspecting the answer. He said it was presented
by the A.R.E. Clinic in Phoenix. I laughingly told him I was
going to work for the A.R.E. in Virginia Beach in March. He
then wanted to know what I would be doing, and I told him.
As surprised at the synchronicity as I, he said he had talked
with some people at the A.R.E. in September about that very
job and was told it had been filled. Because he had connec-
tions and experience which he thought would be helpful to
the A.R.E., he volunteered to help the new person when that
individual arrived. Without Al Miner knowing any of this,
his psychic source had brought us together through a past-
life connection. Maybe it was a coincidence, but the odds
in favor of such an occurrence were astronomical. As we
concluded the phone conversation, we agreed that the Lord
works in mysterious ways. He promised to visit after I got to
Virginia Beach.

I was looking forward to my new job at the A.R.E., but
had many conflicting emotions as I contemplated leaving
Louisville. I had spent fifteen years there. They had been
both exhilarating and traumatic. I had achieved a level of

success at the bank which I hadn't dared to hope for, and I had lost it all, including some of my physical faculties with attendant, constant pain. I also felt that my decision to work for the A.R.E. had been confirmed by the unusual procession of psychic events and synchronistic happenings that had transpired in the past few months.

Just a short time earlier, Hugh Lynn Cayce had come to Louisville on some business and asked me to visit with him in the evening. The previous evening, I had received word from my sister in Hopkinsville that her husband had died from an unexpected heart attack. I needed to go there, of course, but delayed doing so until after my meeting with Hugh Lynn. He simply wanted to talk about aspects of my upcoming job and be sure that I was firm in my decision to accept it. I invited him to go with me to Hopkinsville the next day, which was his birthplace as well as the home of his psychic father. He couldn't believe that I was really going to go there and almost agreed to join me, but his prior commitments prevented it.

While sitting with my family during the funeral services, I wondered anew about relocating to Virginia Beach away from all my relatives and friends. The question was still on my mind as they laid my brother-in-law to rest at the cemetery. After the final graveside prayer, I looked away. There, within sight, was an unpretentious, small, flat gravestone. On it were the names of Edgar Cayce and his wife, Gertrude. I knew I had my answer.

The Study Group Council had a farewell dinner before I left. There were gifts and goodwill messages. I realized this group was, in effect, part of my family that I was leaving. What's more, I had to say good-by to the Webers. Hardest of all, though, was leaving Vickie behind. I think she knew. She didn't want me to get far from her in the last few days. Tom Ballard, with whom she had been thoroughly familiar in her earlier years, had agreed to move back into my apartment and manage the building. He would take good care of her. As I left my apartment to head for Virginia Beach, I looked back before finally shutting the door. Vickie was peering around the corner of the refrigerator with a sad and knowing look on her face. The tears flowed freely as I climbed into my car and headed east.

CHAPTER TWELVE

I began working at the A.R.E. on the last day of March, 1982. By and large, I was welcomed. There were some staff and A.R.E. members, however, who questioned the propriety of embarking on a formal fund-raising program. For me, this issue was resolved by directions reiterated in the Cayce readings themselves to seek financial support from those who had been helped by the information. In this fashion, the appeal would give them an opportunity to put their worldy goods to work in service for others. Beyond this mildly controversial issue, the A.R.E. people were a very warm and wonderful group with which to be identified.

It was a propitious time to be arriving at the A.R.E. The year 1982 would turn out to witness a changing of the guard. The son of Edgar Cayce and Chairman of the Board was Hugh Lynn Cayce, who had almost single-handedly built the A.R.E. into a respected organization with over 20,000 members worldwide. Although his son, Charles Thomas Cayce, had been designated president a few years before, Hugh Lynn's influence was still the guiding force in the organization. His health was not the best, but when I came aboard in March I didn't realize—and probably no one else did at the time—that Hugh Lynn had just slightly more than three months to live and only one month remaining on the job. Another major figure in the organization and probably its chief lecturer and writer, Herbert Puryear, would leave his family and the A.R.E. a month after the death of Hugh Lynn and relocate to Phoenix, Arizona. A fragile period of reorganization and rethinking regarding the direction of the A.R.E. work was at hand.

Hugh Lynn invited me to lunch many times in the three- or four-week period before he entered the hospital. He talked nonstop during these brief moments together. He told me about his personal readings and the early days of the organization, his philosophy, and his hopes for the future. I was honored to be in the presence of this man who had miraculously maintained and expanded an organization after the death of his famous father. Hugh Lynn had brought the information in these psychic readings into the consciousness of the world. This information had left an indelible mark on society's concepts of medicine, prehistory, religion, the nature and purpose of life, and the future. It had brought the subjects of Atlantis, reincarnation, and earth changes into the common parlance of everyday conversation and acceptability. In retrospect, I think that Hugh Lynn's avid and passionate talks with me reflected his conviction that the Office of Development could have an impact on the future of the Cayce work. Furthermore, I believe our talks showed his recognition of his own imminent departure.

Hugh Lynn Cayce died on July 4, 1982. Testimonials poured in from around the world. The local newspaper had a glowing editorial on the significant accomplishments of this man. A moving memorial service was held at the A.R.E. Conference Center auditorium, a building which he had envisioned and brought into existence.

In the midst of all these changes, I jumped into the tasks of my job and the busy summer conference season. By September when the heavy stream of visitors began to diminish, I was nearly exhausted. My leg pains were dissipating my energy. But as things began slowing down, both Charles Thomas Cayce and I concluded that I would be able to handle the demands of my job.

After I had gotten settled into a rented high-rise condominium unit near the Chesapeake Bay, Gary Rose moved into his own apartment in Norfolk, about twenty miles away. Gary had helped me through a difficult period of adjustment to new surroundings and activity. To my relief, I found I could be independent and self-sufficient. He also left solely in my hands the task of completing the book begun on the past lives of Jesus.

In time, I obtained a reading from Anne Puryear, a psychic in Phoenix, Arizona, who married Herb Puryear shortly after his departure from Virginia Beach and his ensuing divorce. I had heard a number of positive testimonials about her ability and was curious how the information might stack up against my readings from Al Miner and others. Her reading supplied an incredible amount of information, especially about past lives. Like Al, she indicated I had assumed the task, before entering this life, to undergo the difficulties during physical embodiment of being shot, partially paralyzed, and coping with pain—all for a spiritual purpose. She gave me a rather tall assignment with the statement, "This one has come to write of his experiences and to bring light and hope and help to those through the sharing of that which has occurred through his life." (See Appendix B.)

The past lives basically agreed with those I had been given earlier by Al Miner, but there was another consistency which really boggled my mind. She also, at the end of the reading, gave the name of Brad, the person in California who had called me upon the recommendation of Al's psychic reading. There certainly was no collaboration between these two, and she hadn't known of these earlier readings from Al, much less what he had said. These facts lent a strong element of veracity to the psychic talent of both individuals. Her reading inspired me to greater effort in dealing with my physical limitations.

About that time I received word that Brad would be visiting. He came by the A.R.E. and gave some helpful advice on running a development office. We had dinner together and shared the experiences each of us had had in this lifetime. I don't think either of us was certain about any past lives together. Nevertheless, we seemed to have an easy camaraderie with each other and were willing to accept such a possibility.

There was another visitor soon thereafter whom I had been looking forward to meeting. Arch Ogden, one of the Edgar Cayce Foundation trustees, told me that Al Miner had come with him to Virginia Beach and that he would be bringing Al by my office. When I met Al, I hesitated. I was certain I had met him before and felt I should indicate that fact. But, of course, I hadn't—at least not in this lifetime. Al told me later that he had felt the same way. The Cayce readings identify this unusual feeling—an inexplicable sense of knowing someone. They call it past-life recognition. Al and I got along quite well and looked forward to future visits together. He told me I was working where I should be and that it was important for me to stay at the A.R.E. It was welcomed advice that confirmed my intentions.

There really was no place I'd rather be than the A.R.E. It was a work that I felt was divinely inspired. The staff and members of the organization were loving and beautiful people. There was a powerful intensity and commitment to the work begun by Edgar Cayce decades earlier.

But at times this dedication could be disruptive. The Cayce readings reached people at many levels and had a message with the potential to unite virtually all faiths and persuasions. Some people became connected with the A.R.E. because of its spiritual concepts, while others were variously intrigued with the information on health, dreams, past civilizations, earth changes, the continuity of life, study groups, or prophecies. Whatever the connection, it often became the individual's primary commitment. Too often, I felt, members became tied to single-issue causes without due regard to the broad overall purpose of the organization. It wasn't possible to be all things to all people, especially with limited resources. Those whose special interests were not fully served sometimes became unhappy and complained loudly.

I was surprised at the difficulty of satisfying our constituency. There were few decisions that met with unanimous acceptance; usually the satisfaction of two people resulted in the dissatisfaction of at least one other. In addition, there were other groups in society who felt an open antagonism with A.R.E.'s programs. Some fundamentalist religious factions, for example, took particular affront at Cayce's infusion of reincarnation into a Christian philosophy of life and spirituality.

Situations such as this type made working for the A.R.E. challenging. One big consolation to me was knowing that this kind of dilemma has probably been the lot of all worthwhile endeavors throughout history. It certainly was the case for Jesus and the early church. It surprised me to discover how many similarities, both in process and belief, exist between the early Christian effort and that of the Edgar Cayce work. The early church resolved the problem of dissenting opinion by a series of councils. They formulated creeds characterizing all divergent ideas and unsanctioned beliefs as heresy and evil. This could be a tempting and easy way out, but I prayed that the A.R.E. would never succumb to such a solution. All persons should be free and open to reach their own conclusions and interpretations about the meaning and validity of the Edgar Cayce readings; there should be no offical line or condemnation of those who differ, particularly in the spiritual arena. The readings insisted upon this openness to all, and I was surprised at how many people claimed the Cayce material had brought them back to organized religion rather than away from it.

I had noticed that television evangelists—and it began to seem like virtually *all* religious speakers—invariably claim they have the "truth." The implication—and one often stated directly—is that those who don't agree with them lack the truth. As a consequence, the term "truth" had come to be one of uncertainty and frustration for me. When I heard the word, it raised a red flag, alerting me to likely intolerance on the part of the speaker.

The psychic readings of Edgar Cayce, however, had a definition of truth which revived my respect and appreciation for the word. In response to the question "What is truth?" the following answer was given in reading 262-81: "That which makes [one] aware of the Divine within each and every activity . . . and is a growth in each and every soul." By this definition, no one could claim to have an exclusive hold on truth. The truth is simply that which brings a person closer to the Divine or God. This concept allows for personal growth without an individual leaving the parameters of truth. In fact, I recognized that my own idea of what was reliable and factual had changed through the years. Yet, if each change had brought me closer to God, it had been truth for me at that time. This definition continues to promote much greater tolerance on my part for others—no matter where they may be on the spiritual path.

A large percentage of the visitors to the A.R.E. were seekers. They were ardently looking for answers to life's many questions. Sometimes the issues were physical or health-related. For others, the search was philosophical or spiritual. Most found answers in the Cayce readings that satisfied their needs and sent them in a new direction with help and hope. It was a joy to watch and to be a part of this process.

I discovered early on that some of the seekers had suffered broken marriages or unhappy love affairs. They were lonely and hurting; they were searching for something to fill the void in their hearts. As a bachelor, I received a fair share of attention from some of these female pilgrims. I cannot deny enjoying this situation. Surprisingly, I found that some were drawn to me because of my physical limitations, which seemed to bring out their motherly instincts. One stated, "Glenn, I want to look after you and take care of you for the rest of your life." A few were convinced they could heal me. It wasn't just an ego trip for me, however. I could empathize with their loneliness and thirst for affection and love. But I found there was a tightrope I had to walk. While I wanted to share my care and concern and to extend love in a nonattached manner, I didn't want to mislead or hurt anyone if I felt no romantic attraction. There had been a time in my life when I might have taken advantage of such situations, but I had in recent years set an ideal of permitting intimacy and sexual involvement only as a complement to genuine love from the heart. There were many temptations, but I had learned to live within this ideal. The potential consequences of doing otherwise outweighed all other considerations.

The sexual force is a powerful influence in each individual's life, and it appears that everyone has a different rule or standard to apply. A Cayce reading, again, had been very helpful in guiding me along this path.

Know, all the desires ... have their place in thy experience. These are to be used and not abused. All things are holy unto the Lord, that He has given to man as appetites or physical desires, yet these are to be used to the glory of God and not in that direction of selfishness alone. 3234-1

Although what constitutes abuse and selfishness remains a subjective standard which undoubtedly will vary with individuals, still this advice seems to be timely and appropriate for today's sensually oriented society.

I now felt at home in Virginia Beach and considered myself an active part of the A.R.E. headquarters activity. It seemed symbolic, then, when sometime in the fall, I received word that Vickie, my dog back in Kentucky, had died. Her departure formally closed a major chapter in my life. I was now fully embarked upon and involved in the next one.

CHAPTER THIRTEEN

January 8, 1984, the tenth anniversary of my shooting, found me in Egypt. I was part of an A.R.E. tour group, which was spending nearly three weeks exploring the sights of this ancient country. We spent a full week floating down the Nile River from Aswan to Cairo on a boat chartered exclusively for our approximately 100 participants.

I never thought, especially during my long period of recuperation, that I could ever attempt anything as rigorous as traveling to and through Egypt. There were times on the trip that I was convinced I should have stayed home, such as when climbing up into the King's Chamber of the Great Pyramid and when walking a plank from a felucca boat on the Nile to the shore at Aswan. All in all, however, it was a great trip which acquainted me with significant sites featured in the Cayce readings and which brought back to me what I considered to be some fresh past-life memories.

The trip actually was made possible by a gift from a former study group member. Marjorie had been one of those members who had come to the rehabilitation center and stood by my bed as the group concluded its meetings with meditation and prayer. She had lent encouragement and hope during the many days of my recovery. Her support was typical of what I had received from all the group members. I was informed before the trip to Egypt of her death and that she had left a bequest to me in her will. It was nearly enough to pay for the trip's cost.

Catherine, Margie's friend and my former study group dream interpreter, sent me a book of unpublished poems, which she had found in Margie's personal effects. She thought maybe the A.R.E. would want them because some of the poems related to trips Margie had made to Virginia Beach to attend A.R.E. conferences. I read the entire collection and found one that particularly moved me. It was dated February 1974 and said:

> For Glenn
>
> Thank You
> Thank You, loving Lord, dear God
> For listening to our prayer.
> Now that his life's certain
> Our hearts are light as air.
> How wonderful again
> To know that Thou art there.

Such is the loving care I had found in a Search for God study group. The group experience had truly shaped and affected my life, as I know it had for the others. It is something I wouldn't be without and why I still participate in such a group today.

And, as an unexpected bonus, I was in Egypt.

I had come to believe that synchronicity—meaningful coincidence—often can be a source of guidance from God. I think it's important to make a decision, pray and meditate about it, and then look for dreams or other guidance, such as little events of synchronicity, which support or oppose the decision.

The famous Swiss psychologist, Carl Jung, attached great significance to synchronicity and the coincidences that can signify its presence:

The more they [coincidences] multiply and the

greater and more exact the correspondence is, the more their probability sinks and their unthinkability increases, until they can no longer be regarded as pure chance but, for lack of a causal explanation, have to be thought of as meaningful arrangements. (Jung, *Synchronicity: An Acausal Connecting Principle*)

In the case of Egypt, I felt I was surely supposed to go. While contemplating the decision, I kept hearing of friends who planned to be a part of the tour. Several people I worked with at the A.R.E. were going, including my close friend Anne Hunt. Then I learned that a number of my Louisville A.R.E. friends had decided to go, and among them was Lynn Weber. In addition, two old friends from college sent in their registrations. One of them, Emmabelle, had dated a fraternity brother and was a close friend of a young woman I had dated. The other had been a counselor to my small orientation group when I entered college. He had a distinguished career in law school and as a campus leader and had been my role model. This supporting cast and other meaningful coincidences convinced me I was supposed to use Margie's gift to go to Egypt. There also would be the prospect of three days in Greece—the country that had held so many haunting memories for me several years before.

Some of the most exciting information in the Edgar Cayce readings pertained to Egypt. According to Cayce, in the period around 10,500 B.C., Egypt had been one of the areas to which refugees from the legendary continent of Atlantis had come in anticipation of the destruction of their homeland. They had brought with them vestiges of their advanced civilization and had been involved in the building of the Great Pyramid and the Sphinx, both of which reputedly had been the repository of artifacts or writings reflecting ancient history and making prophecies even about our times. One of the key figures of the time had been a priest named Ra Ta, who, the readings claimed, had been an incarnation of Edgar Cayce. Many of the people associated with Cayce had also lived at the time of Ra Ta, and this had an important relevance and bearing upon the present. Traditional dating of both the Sphinx and the Great Pyramid points to construction much later than Cayce's psychically perceived timetable. But recent exploration and research raise the possibility that Cayce, not the scientific archaeologists, are more accurate. It was thus a tremendous thrill to be at those ancient sites and speculate on the possibilities of the past.

Shortly before leaving for Egypt, I dreamed that I was in a boat floating down the Nile and could see the Great Pyramid in the distance. It was under construction with huge earthen ramps and wood scaffolding leading around and to the top of the pyramid. Anne Hunt was with me in the boat, and we seemed to share a close rapport. Sometime after this dream I received interesting confirmation. Archaeologist Mark Lehner, who was doing research for the Edgar Cayce Foundation when we were there, told me that he had found definite evidence of such ramps and scaffolding in the area around the pyramid. Because of the strong feeling I had for Anne, I suspected the dream was also indicating past-life involvement between us. The psychic readings from Al Miner and Anne Puryear had both indicated that I had been a follower of Ra Ta's and that I was present as the pyramid was being built. In any event, the dream was a nice prelude to the trip and left me with a warm respect and feeling for ancient Egypt.

Another important consideration for me was being in the land where the biblical Joseph had risen from servitude to becoming second-in-command to the pharaoh. From my study of the past lives of Jesus according to Cayce, I knew that Joseph reputedly had been a significant one of those incarnations.

During the trip I experienced an inner confirmation of my own connection with these times. Just a few hours on the Nile downriver from Aswan, I was sitting on the top deck of the boat and idly looking at the passing scenery to the west. In something like a state of reverie, I was suddenly transported back in time and seemed to be checking crops that were growing in the area I was viewing. I was working for Joseph and knew that it was my duty to report to him the extent and condition of these crops. As soon as my conscious mind realized the significance of my thoughts and images, they ceased, and I was back in the present. I felt certain from the strength of this flashback that I had really been alive at the time of Joseph and had worked under him in his program to monitor and collect surplus harvest.

But my most memorable experience of this nature occurred at Tell el Amarna, the city of Ikhnaton, also known as Pharaoh Amenhotep IV. Again I seemed to be transported back in time and could "see" Jacob and Joseph's brothers coming around a bend in the Nile River to the north on their way to visit Joseph at Amarna. I was convinced that Ikhnaton was the legendary pharaoh who had been friendly to Joseph and that this city was where so much of the biblical Joseph story had taken place. Although a few researchers support this scenario, the conventional view is that the Joseph period occurred 100 or more years earlier. Nevertheless, my flashbacks remained for me a powerful and personal connection with Egypt and with Joseph.

While I had enjoyed my stay in Egypt, it was Greece once again that truly brought a sense of identity and exhilaration. The last three days of the tour were spent there, primarily in the Athens area, although one day involved a cruise to nearby islands, which were extremely beautiful. Everywhere we went, sites seemed familiar and full of rapport for me. I was particularly moved by the picturesque quaintness of the island and harbor of Poros. I vowed to return there someday. Even the Grecian sunsets seemed to have special meaning and poignancy.

The last evening in Greece was my birthday. I couldn't help recalling this day ten years before in Norton Hospital. Although dinner on this evening was quite tasty, it could never rival that beef-tomato soup served to me in the hospital!

We flew back to the United States the next morning. I found myself thinking back on the details of both the Greek and Egyptian portions. The tour had been something quite special, and I learned the value of traveling with A.R.E. people. Not only were they unusually pleasant and considerate, their interests generally coincided with mine. Our local tour guide, Ahmed Fayed, was not only well respected in his native country but had spent several summers working at Virginia Beach with A.R.E. visitors. He was assisted by Mark Lehner, who shared insights from his archaeological work in Egypt. It was great having guides who, when pointing out sights to see, would add comments about what the Cayce readings had stated concerning the history of each place. But most important for me were the lasting friendships I acquired with so many of my fellow travelers.

That adventure of January, 1984, made deep impressions on me. But exactly a year later, I was in a hospital again. The cause was unexpected and a little bizarre.

A Saturday evening in early January, Gary Rose dropped by for a visit. I had just poured the last of my holiday-season eggnog into a glass and was returning to resume watching television with him. Suddenly there was a pop, I felt a dizzy swaying, and my right leg buckled under me. Eggnog and glass went flying. I went down on my right leg, which ended up doubled under me. I realized that my leg brace had given way, then I discovered that the brace was broken on both sides. I straightened my leg out, fearing it too might be broken. As I examined my leg more closely, I saw that it was quite bad: Not just a cracked bone as had happened several years before, but I could move my lower leg freely in any direction without any effect on the upper part. The leg bone apparently was broken entirely at a spot about three inches above the knee.

I was despondent, almost hysterically so, as I contemplated the consequences: another hospital stay, inability to get around for no telling how long, absence from work, more pain—the list seemed endless and overwhelming. Gary called for an ambulance, then brought out my suitcase and the items to go in it, which I knew from experience were hospital necessities.

In thirty minutes, I was at the emergency room of Virginia Beach General Hospital and was x-rayed shortly thereafter. The femur—the thigh bone—had a jagged and total break, just as I had anticipated. My doctor, hastily summoned from his home, told me I had two choices: having my leg put in traction for four to six months or having a steel plate surgically inserted and fastened to the broken bone ends. I would be able to get up and out on crutches in a week or two with the latter procedure. By now, surgery was "old hat," so the choice was easy. The plate was implanted in my thigh the next morning.

When I called back to Kentucky to let my friends know of my latest escapade, the response was automatic. Tom Ballard would come and help me during my first week out of the hospital; Lynn Weber would come the second week. By then, I should be able to return to work.

That was exactly the way things turned out! Both Tom and Lynn had to brave snow and slick roads through West Virginia, but their loyalty, caring, and help were of inestimable value. Again, former study group friends were extending fellowship and love to me.

I was back at work in just over two weeks, my mobility reduced, but at least I was present with the aid of crutches.

Several people suggested I should sue the company that had made the brace for me. It had been constructed only a few months before, and the thickest steel hadn't been used to prepare the brace. However, it shouldn't have broken, and the company representatives admitted as much. They were quick to visit me at the hospital and to begin work on a replacement. I probably could have prevailed in a lawsuit, but—and it may not sound like a lawyer speaking—I just didn't feel right in such a course of action. The people at the brace company had always been helpful and accommodating to me. If they had made any kind of mistake or been negligent, it was unintentional. Besides, I was thankful I hadn't been sued for every mistake I had made in life. Maybe I would have looked at the situation differently had my hospitalization insurance not covered the medical expenses. Certainly there had been pain and suffering from the injury, but they were no strangers to me by now. In later months and years, as I had further dealings with the company and its people, I was very glad they were still my friends and that I hadn't tried to exact everything I could from them.

I searched hard to find some hidden blessing in this apparent misfortune. Maybe it was the new car I ended up buying. Mine began acting up when I returned to work, and I knew I was in no condition to be stranded without transportation. A car was my legs and means of participation in life around me. A fellow employee, Joan Grasser, learned of my predicament, and her daughter who worked at an auto dealership selected a salesman to come by and visit me at work. Three days later, he delivered the new car I had decided upon and drove my old one away. He had even taken care of its licensing and installation of the hand-driving controls which I required. I had a much more dependable means of transportation now, and the purchase of a new car and trade-in of the old one couldn't have been accomplished any easier or better—all thanks to my injury and crutches.

Maybe serendipity was brewing in the medical advice I had received from one of my doctors about a physician at Duke University who dealt with spinal-injury pain control. I got in touch with him. His proposed solution was to cut the specific nerves in the spinal cord which go to my painful leg areas. When the bullet had been removed from my spine eleven years before, this operation had been mentioned as a future option. I needed to know more about the procedure and possible consequences before seriously considering it as a solution now, however.

Perhaps in the meantime I would get that healing I had been searching and waiting for for so long. I hadn't given up on this hope.

CHAPTER FOURTEEN

I finished my book on the previous lives of Jesus in September, 1987. It had been a long and arduous undertaking for me, requiring a great amount of research. But I was pleased with one result: I had found considerable support from various ancient sources corroborating Edgar Cayce's claims about earlier appearances of the soul we know as Jesus. During my eight years of research and writing, a number of highly relevant new books and English translations became available—ones about the Dead Sea Scrolls and documents found at Nag Hammadi, Egypt. All of them had material on the past-life subject. I also concluded after intensive research into early Christianity that Edgar Cayce had enunciated and recovered some of the teachings of Jesus that had been virtually lost in antiquity—lost by censorship and various biblical translations.

Had Edgar Cayce actually helped me from the other side as I had been promised? I'm inclined to think that he did but cannot, of course, prove it. There were many times when ideas or ways of phrasing concepts seemed to come from "out of the blue." There were also a couple of nighttime experiences, when I was awakened from sleep, for which I have no logical explanation. Two events especially stand out.

The first occurred during the period while writing about

Zend, a supposed past life of Jesus. I woke up one night with the word "Parsee" on my lips. Zend lived in Persia and was the father of the religious leader Zoroaster. I learned later that Parsee is the name by which the Persian Zoroastrians are known today in India, their last remaining refuge.

The most helpful experience had to do with the biblical Joshua, who, Cayce claimed, was also an earlier life of Jesus. I had trouble with Joshua because of his bloody wars of conquest in the Israelite Promised Land. The Cayce readings even said that one should study the life of Joshua to understand Jesus' life. I couldn't imagine how this could be so, and, after starting the Joshua chapter of my book, I became stymied and went on to other chapters. One Saturday night I awoke with these words ringing in my ears: "Look at where Joshua killed and Jesus healed." The next morning I checked Bible maps of Joshua's military campaigns alongside maps of Jesus' ministry. They were essentially one and the same. Where Joshua killed, Jesus restored life and health. This was a vital key in understanding the significance of the Joshua lifetime.

I thus truly felt that I had been helped from the other side, including other incidents when my leg pains made writing and concentration difficult, but unexpected relief would come from somewhere.

Through the years, my leg pains had lessened somewhat, but they still controlled my day. I had learned to enjoy life despite the pain, and I had learned a lot about it. The pain in both legs below the knees never went away, but it did have great variations. Very early on I learned that there was a two-day cycle in which one day saw a sharp, burning pain and the next day was more of a drawing, tensing pain—like a spring wound too tightly. Also, each day provided many ups and downs, punctuated by climactic spasming of the muscles, similar to a "charley horse" but worse. There would then be a reduced period of pain followed by a gradual buildup again, until the leg spasms returned. This cycle continued on and on throughout each day and night. In the daytime, these severe spasms typically occurred about every fifteen minutes. Even sleep at night was periodically interrupted by these peak episodes of pain. The worst times, though, were occasional days when the buildup of pain just continued, and the leg muscles didn't spasm to provide a release.

I tried to watch for patterns and possible causes of these variations, but they never seemed to be consistent. The only exceptions were weather changes, particularly wet and humid weather, when the pains were always worse. Standing or being in any position for some length of time also increased the pain. I had found one position that generally lessened the pain for a time: to lie face down briefly across a bed with my legs extending over the side. Maybe it was a sort of reverse tension and pull on the leg muscles and nerves. But whatever, it usually provided some relief. It was significant enough that I purchased a couch without sidearms for my office so that I could get periods of reduced pain at work.

The net result of all this was a limited life style, affected more by pain than by the paralysis of my right leg, which mildly hampered walking and general mobility. The pain was insidious and energy depleting. Also, it wasn't something other people could observe and be aware of; that is, until leg spasms sent me into strange grimaces and contortions. Strangers often wondered what was going on, and a waitress in one restaurant once summoned a doctor, thinking I was having either an epileptic seizure or a heart attack. One doctor likened the intensity of my pains to that of childbirth in women.

I tried various prescribed medications and drugs, but nothing helped. During my early days after being shot, the doctors administered both codeine and morphine with totally negligible results. Maybe the lack of drug relief was good; at least I hadn't become addicted to nor dependent upon any chemical formulation or substance.

Life, of course, went on. I tried to keep a smile on my face when I was around others, even when the pain seemed overwhelming. I wondered if those around me had any idea how much pain I was experiencing most of the time, but I preferred to endure the pain as privately as possible. Aside from the pain itself, there were activities I regretted not being able to do. I had to avoid crowds or any situation which required much walking or standing. Even simple social events, such as a dinner out, could sometimes be unpleasant. But I think it was the inability to take long hikes and enjoy the beauty of nature that bothered me most. Nevertheless, I could work at being either happy or miserable, a decision which would also affect others around me. A Cayce reading put the challenge this way:

> Thus ye may find in thy mental and spiritual self, ye can make thyself just as happy or just as miserable as ye like. How miserable do ye want to be?   2995-3

From the beginning, I tried to make it through each day, one at a time. I assumed that the pains would diminish and go away reasonably soon. I'm not sure I could have handled it during those early days had I known what really lay ahead. There were some improvements, but not enough to make life anything close to comfortable. I still had probably as much pain in a twenty-four-hour period as I had had in all my life before being shot. Thus, I continued to seek every possible means of relief.

Conventional medicine hadn't supplied the solution for me, at least one for which the risks seemed acceptable, so I kept looking for possible nonconventional answers, including psychic healers. I had tried to follow the healing advice of my psychic readings, but doing so hadn't produced observable progress. Sometimes the psychic information didn't give enough specific detail so that I could be certain that I had employed the correct procedures. For example, the first Al Miner reading had suggested using the Wet-Cell Appliance that Edgar Cayce had first recommended for certain individuals. Whereas the Cayce readings prescribed various spots for connecting the device to the body, the Al Miner reading didn't direct me to specific spots for my condition. I was never sure that I used it properly for my particular affliction.

But the main problem was the sheer scope of the treatments. From diet, medications, electrical appliances, castor oil packs, daily massages, and other procedures, I had no time for anything else. The Puryear reading added further complicated tasks. The treatments were simply overwhelming; I tried the recommended regimens for three months and then gave up in frustration. I couldn't hold a job and continue these treatments which were thus far unsuccessful.

In late August, 1986, I heard reports about a Philippine psychic surgeon who was visiting the Virginia Beach area. My study group members encouraged me to go to him and actually paid for my visit. It was an unbelievable experience.

Alex Orbito was doing his surgery and healing in a private home, and I went there in the early afternoon with some trepidation. There was already a crowd in the living room, and I heard glowing accounts of his healing and surgery sessions that had occurred that morning. I had to fill out some forms, and I received instructions on what I would need to do after receiving my treatment. Eventually it came my time to enter the "operating room." The walls were festooned with pictures of Jesus and the Virgin Mary. A fairly young Filipino man greeted me in accented English.

"What is your problem?"

I told him about my spinal injury, paralysis, and pain. He told me to take off my shirt and lie face down on a massage table in the center of the room. I then felt his hand over the spot where the bullet had hit my spine and heard him gently praying. It then seemed that he scraped his fingernail along my spinal column. There was no pain as I felt his hand rubbing further at the injury site. I realized he was throwing something in a small plastic bucket, and then I felt his hand rub gently from the top to the bottom of my back and spine. After no more than three or four minutes, he said I could get up. His female assistant was wiping blood from my back as I sat up on the side of the table and saw reddish-black bits of flesh or blood clots in the plastic bucket. I realized they had come from my body. He told me not to get my back wet for twenty-four hours and suggested I have a few more sessions with him. For the next twenty-four hours or so, a slight red scar, where my incision had been made, remained visible. Eventually it disappeared.

When I returned to the waiting room, I learned that my experience was similar to that of others who had had treatment from Orbito.

A little later, several of us were allowed to witness his surgery on three other patients. After concentrating his healing energy over the area of a patient, he passed his hand or finger across the skin, and in doing so appeared to make some kind of incision through which his hand could enter the body. Black or dark-red flesh material, similar to that taken from me, was then withdrawn from the body and discarded. A small amount of blood usually flowed from the opened area. At the conclusion, Orbito passed his hand over the opening, and the skin sealed tightly shut. I witnessed this "surgical" procedure on numerous people, and later was able to videotape some of it. Many patients reported immediate relief from various ailments, including eye problems, arthritis, diabetes, chronic back pain, and even cancer.

I had three sessions with him but experienced no improvement in my pain or paralysis. Nevertheless, I came away with a healthy respect for his ability. To this day I don't understand what I saw, but I'm totally convinced there was no fraud or fakery involved. It just wouldn't have been possible under the circumstances. I also saw several of my friends, whose veracity and credibility were unquestioned, come away healed. The surgeon was extremely pious and sincere, praying quietly before and at the end of each treatment. I had witnessed miracles, even though I hadn't been one of them.

One Sunday evening in late September, I woke up and unconsciously rubbed my right hip which was itching. Suddenly I realized there were feeling and sensation where there had been none before. Could I be imagining this? No, I definitely had new feeling in my right hip. The next morning, it was confirmed when the itch returned. It had been approximately a month since my sessions with the psychic surgeon, and I was truly able to ascertain there was a reduction of paralysis. I had feeling where I had had none before. It was a miracle, and it was happening to me!

I told a few close friends what was occurring, but generally tried to be low-keyed about the whole thing until the healing was more complete and apparent to everyone who saw me.

The return, although slow, was still continuing when the new year arrived, and I decided to start writing about all that had happened to me since being shot, while it was still relatively fresh in my mind. After all, several psychic readings had counseled me to write or tell of my experiences and that that was part of the reason I had been injured. I thus began working on this narrative.

During the spring, I obtained another psychic reading. It was from Wes Setliff, or Joshua John-David, as his psychic source addressed him. He had moved to Virginia Beach, and a good friend whose judgment I respected worked with him and spoke highly of his psychic ability. I was present when Wes went into trance and began answering the questions I had prepared and now read to him.

He said my healing was made possible by completing the book on Jesus, which was finished in September—the very month I had first discovered some return of feeling. My injury, he said, was brought on in part to assure that I would write the book and also in order for me to be in a proper mental and emotional state to relate better to a suffering messiah. Now that the work was completed, I could be healed, and he foresaw that happening.

Wes also identified most of the lifetimes which Al Miner and Anne Puryear had previously described for me. He added that because of my minority position at the Council of Nicaea, I had subsequently been put on a wheel or rack of torture in an attempt to force a recantation of my beliefs about Jesus. As a result, I died after my spine was cracked at the same spot where I was shot this lifetime. The similar injury now helped put me in the vibration of those Nicaean days so that I could more clearly write of the beliefs my soul had once held but couldn't publicly espouse.

The way that this psychic reading fit together the pieces of my soul's experience was awesome. I had no idea whether or not it was true, but I was impressed with other answers Wes gave—answers which could more easily be verified. The fact that his description of my past lives matched those received from others augered well for his credibility. On the one hand, I feared focusing too much on previous lives. But the concept of reincarnation and what I had been told about it lent support and possible meaning to what was happening to me in this lifetime. It made everything sound as if order and purpose do guide the universe and that serendipity really is present and available.

I was scheduled to speak at the annual A.R.E. Congress in

June, 1988, about my book *Lives of the Master,* which had now been published by the A.R.E. Press. I decided to tell the gathering what Wes had said in his reading about the connection between writing the book and being healed. I also shared with them the fact that I had received some healing and return of feeling as well as my expectations for a total recovery. The group was excited and rejoiced with me in this miraculous turn of events.

Later in the summer I reluctantly had to conclude that the healing had ceased. There had been no observable return for some months now. I hadn't lost the recovered feeling in my right leg, but it just hadn't continued long enough to result in significant new use of my leg. I still required the full-length leg brace.

Why had I even gotten a healing, I wondered, if it was to be so limited? I regretted having told anyone, especially the Congress audience, of the short miracle I had experienced. I had been motivated by a desire to give testimony regarding my blessing and to follow through on the directives from my psychic readings to tell others of my experiences. But to my audiences would it not appear that I had tried to be overly sensational, projecting unrealistic hopes and expectations far too early?

But why had the healing stopped? If the early healing had been the result of answered prayer and a gift from God, had I done something wrong to cause it to stop? Or did the orderly and purposeful universe I had come to believe in have some lesson for me to learn from this stop-and-go experience? I didn't know the answers to these questions. I only knew that I was deeply disappointed but not yet willing to give up on my hopes for being healed.

The psychic surgeon returned to Virginia Beach, and I had several more sessions with him and then again the following year. But on these occasions there was no apparent healing.

As I reflected on the situation, I wondered if I had been correct in giving credit to the psychic surgeon for my limited healing. I remembered that a few weeks before his original visit, I had had a session with Ethel Lombardi, a well-known and successful healer who did most of her treatment without physically touching the patient. She had been at the A.R.E. as part of a health conference and volunteered to work with me. The session had lasted nearly two hours, and I did feel some sensation as she tried to send energy through my spinal cord. At first there was a block, presumably at the injury site, but then I could feel a warmth go all the way to my toes. Maybe she was the one who had triggered some return of feeling several weeks later.

Despite the discouraging turn of events, all I knew to do was to keep trying for further relief from wherever it might come.

I took another look at the possibility of having the nerves cut which go to the pain-affected areas of my legs. The doctor at Duke University said that the risk of losing any function, other than pain sensation, was minimal. I talked to Dr. Norman Shealy, whose pain clinic I had once attended. He recommended against the operation, claiming that while it is irreversible, the pain loss, even if successful, often ends after a time. Dr. William McGarey, of the A.R.E. Clinic in Phoenix, Arizona, similarly had reservations about the procedure.

Some years before, I had joined the Spinal Cord Society, a national organization devoted to seeking a cure for spinal-injury paralysis. When they first began their efforts, medical authorities were virtually unanimous in the conclusion that nerves, and especially those of the central nervous system, couldn't be regrown or rejuvenated. In some part due to the research efforts of the Spinal Cord Society, this opinion had been greatly modified. Under certain conditions in the laboratory and in animal experiments, central nervous system tissue had been regrown. In fact, the current prospects look encouraging for the elimination of paralysis from spinal cord injuries in the not-too-distant future. This possibility was another factor to consider in connection with cutting nerves to eliminate my pain, especially since cutting is final and permanent. In view of the uncertainties, I decided definitely against the nerve-cutting procedure.

The Spinal Cord Society did suggest two or three doctors I might want to contact regarding my pain. One was at Baltimore's Johns Hopkins Hospital, which was only a five-hour drive from Virginia Beach. Eventually an appointment was set up for me in January, 1989.

After very thorough examinations in January and a return trip in April, my doctor recommended spinal implant surgery. Wiring would be put into my body along the spine. When activated by an external control, it would send a mild electrical current to my lower legs where I experienced pain. It would, it was hoped, override some or all of the pain. The physicians claimed that the prospects of eliminating or reducing my pain were good, probably in the eighty percent range. I quickly agreed to the procedure, and surgery was set for late June. Because of emergencies greater than mine, it had to be delayed until early July.

My old study group friends came to my assistance again. Tom Ballard came to Virginia Beach and drove me to the hospital in Baltimore. I had to stay awake during the operation so I could tell the doctor the location of the implant which sent the greatest charge to my legs when current was applied. A couple of days of recuperation and learning to use the control box followed, and the pain did appear to be somewhat lessened.

After my surgery, Lynn Weber and her soon-to-be husband, Bob, came to Baltimore and drove me home. My spirits were high on the return journey to Virginia Beach. It was a beautiful summer day, and we went by way of Annapolis, the Naval Academy, and the Eastern Shore of Virginia. The surgery was over, and, although I was still sore, I now had the means to reduce my pain to some extent.

Unfortunately, my euphoria was short-lived. After I got back to Virginia Beach and used the controls for the electrical stimulator, I could feel nothing. Actually, the same result had occurred Saturday morning before I left the hospital, but there had been so many details to attend to in checking out that I didn't pay much attention to the situation. I worked unsuccessfully with the apparatus all weekend.

On Monday, I called Johns Hopkins and talked to my doctor's aide. Over the telephone, he gave some suggestions, but they too failed to send any current which I could feel to my legs. He scheduled me for a return on Friday to see what was wrong.

I drove back to Baltimore on Friday and went through several tests and an x-ray. Afterward my doctor gave me the results.

"Well, I've got good news and bad news."

"What does that mean?" I cautiously asked.

"Your machine works fine, but the implant has pulled loose."

"Is there any way to get it back in place?"

"Not without surgery," he replied.

"How did it happen, and might it not happen again?" I wondered out loud.

"Your spine is very supple, and you can bend over as well as anyone I have ever seen. I think it must have pulled out when you bent over and before the healing was far enough along. We will take extra precautions next time to be sure it cannot pull loose even if you turn somersaults."

There had seemed to be some relief during that short span when the device worked properly. I had come this far and did not want to give up now. It really was an easy decision for me.

"How soon can we do it again?" I questioned. The earliest that surgery could be scheduled again was two weeks later.

My spirits on the return journey home this time stood in sharp contrast to the buoyancy I had felt a week before. Why did it always seem as if I almost got some relief or healing but not quite? Was it my fault? What was I doing wrong? The traffic gridlock around Washington, D.C., on the way home did nothing to improve my mood nor my leg pains, which increase when I am sitting in a car that is not moving. The motion of a car, when moving, usually triggered muscle spasms which, when over, resulted in a significant reduction of pain.

I drove back to Baltimore two weeks later. The operation went routinely, and after three days I drove home to Virginia Beach alone, except for the presence of additional pain from the recent surgery. This time the implant held.

The electrical stimulator really did provide some relief from my pain. It was far from gone, but there was probably a ten to fifteen percent reduction. While that may not sound like much, it was the top end of the pain, and its loss was certainly welcomed. It was now easier to sit through meetings and do other things which required my being in one position for some time. There would be times later when the pain seemed unbearable, and I would wonder if the machine was helpful. But those doubts would quickly vanish when the battery went dead; I couldn't wait to get a replacement.

I now felt that a small but positive and tangible step had been taken along the road which I had hoped would lead to the end of my night of travail.

CHAPTER FIFTEEN

Many other changes were going on in my life during the last half of the 1980s—along with my efforts to find a healing.

It was March 31, 1986, my fourth anniversary date of employment with the A.R.E. when I received a call early Monday morning from a hospital in Kentucky telling me that my mother had died. I had never experienced the death of a close family member or friend, and I wondered how I would emotionally handle such a loss.

My initial reaction was disbelief. Surely there was some mistake. Mother had suffered a heart attack nearly two weeks before, but there had been great improvement since then. She had been moved from the Cardiac Care Unit to a private room, and I had talked with her by phone on Easter Sunday, the day before. She sounded like her old self, and I related a dream I had had about her.

In the dream, Mother had been lying unconscious on a street in Louisville near where I used to live. I found her there, but she soon revived and was doing well. At the end of the dream, she was at a nearby school and seemed to be a student there. In our phone conversation, I told Mother that I was sure the dream was saying she would recover totally and return to life's learning experiences. She seemed satisfied with the interpretation but told me she was ready to go if that was God's will.

I then learned from her that a major heart operation was recommended and had been tentatively scheduled for later in the week. Her doctor felt she couldn't return to an active life without the surgery, although there was some risk to it. She asked me what I thought she should do, and I quickly said I preferred that she do whatever was necessary so she could enjoy her remaining years. She again said she wasn't afraid of death and was prepared for it. She died that night in her sleep from congestive heart failure.

On the trip back to Kentucky and through the wake and funeral, there were sadness and occasional tears on my part. The most difficult moment was when I first saw Mother lying in her coffin. I had a feeling—like a stab in the heart—when I realized that this is *my mother*. It was a personal hurt that I had never known before.

By and large, though, Mother's death wasn't as difficult as I had feared it might be. She had lived an active life, traveling to Florida with my father on vacation just the month before. She didn't have to undergo a long period of suffering or disability, which can often be the lot of the elderly. She was spared the anguish of a surgical operation later in the week. She was ready to go, and her death had been peaceful.

My belief in the continuity of life, however, really eased the burden. Many sources had said the same things about the soul's survival: the Cayce readings and other psychic material, spiritualist contact from the other side which I had witnessed, and the reports of near-death experiences. In fact, their information was eerily similar in detail. I was totally convinced that my mother now was very much alive on another plane of existence—freed from pain and the difficulties of life—and that she was probably enjoying a reunion with loved ones who had preceded her. She was continuing her spiritual journey and growth in a new and different learning level. I felt that I now understood the meaning of the school in my dream, and it was reassuring.

There were some brighter notes to the year, however.

I met Patty at a picnic dinner at the farm home of Charles Thomas Cayce. What originally impressed me most about her was her voice. She sang at the request of several people there, playing her guitar as an accompaniment. Her music was quite beautiful, and I realized she was, too, as I studied her features and watched her soul shine through everything she did. I learned that this was the musician about whom I had heard many recent compliments. She was at the A.R.E. for several weeks during the summer of 1986 to provide musical entertainment and inspiration for those attending our conferences.

Later that evening, I talked with her. She was from Oregon and was a teacher and part-time professional entertainer. I flirted some with her, and she delightfully flirted back.

During the next few weeks I attended every one of her morning musical performances at the A.R.E. Conference Center. We went to dinner, shopping, and movies together on several occasions. Then suddenly it was time for Patty to end her five-week stay and return home.

During her last weekend, we spent a lot of time together. We went to Williamsburg and toured other local sites. I realized that I didn't want her to leave.

I took Patty to the airport to catch her flight home. We had some extra time, and we both opened up and talked freely and seriously with each other.

"Patty, I'm not ready for you to leave," I began.

"I don't want to leave yet either, but I have to," she replied.

I finally admitted to her that I had grown to love and care for her, although I was still sorting out and discovering the depth of my feelings.

"I know," she answered, "I feel the same way. I came here to visit the A.R.E. and have a pleasant vacation at the beach. I got more than I bargained for."

I was thankful that she felt much the same way I did. But what were we to do about it? She was leaving. I knew she had been dating seriously someone in Oregon but had cooled the relationship for the summer to evaluate her true feelings for him. What would happen when she was back there with him? Yet I still wasn't sure of my feelings. I really wasn't ready for any permanent commitment, and she wasn't either.

Neither of us was sure as well on what note we should part. Finally, there was a warm, emotional, and affectionate parting hug and kiss. I had a lump in my throat as I watched her walk away with her guitar case firmly clutched in her right hand. I wondered if I would ever see her again.

As I drove back to work, I couldn't avoid thinking, "Well, it's the same old story again. Just as I get interested and emotionally involved, she goes back to an old boyfriend." The pattern seemed destined to continue forever, and it was painful. I was happy before she arrived, but lonely and hurting now that I had gotten to know her and she was gone. I felt that I would have been better off if we had never met. It seemed simpler and easier for me at the moment to become socially reclusive and avoid any future injuries to the heart.

We wrote each other and talked occasionally over the phone during the next several months. She had resumed her relationship with her boyfriend but wanted to retain a close and special friendship with me. I wasn't pleased with this turn of events but had learned in the past to accept disappointment, put feelings aside, and go on living. I did so again, totally burying the deep feelings I had had at least once for Patty.

Then, nearly two years later, Patty wrote that she was

coming back for four or five weeks in the summer to provide music again for A.R.E. conferences. She asked me to meet her at the airport. I had mixed emotions as I contemplated being with her again. I wanted to see her, but the hurt was now behind me; I didn't want to go through that experience again. But when I met her, I realized some of the old feeling was still there. Her comments didn't help any.

"Glenn, I had to come back and take another look at how I feel about you. I have been confused and uncertain every since I was here."

Although she was still dating her boyfriend, she said she couldn't go on with him without reassessing our relationship.

I was both thrilled and frightened. How did I feel about her now? Did I dare drop my protective guard and let love creep in again?

The next three or four weeks were pleasant and passed quickly, and we decided to take a short trip to Kentucky. I wanted to take her to some of the sites that were dear to me. We both wanted to spend some time together, really getting to know each other, and—we hoped—getting in touch with our true feelings.

We had a wonderful time. She enjoyed the outdoor musical drama, "The Stephen Foster Story," at Bardstown. She appreciated natural beauty as much as I, and she fell in love with Lake Cumberland and Yahoo Falls as I had years before. But I think it was the openness with her that I enjoyed most.

Patty was continually coming up with a game or something fun to do. Sometimes it was just a contest to see who could count the most different kinds of animals we passed as we drove along. At other times, there was more in-depth sharing. She said that friends and lovers become vulnerable and closer by telling things to each other which they would share with no one else. We took turns telling "secrets" from the past. I told her things I never expected to reveal to anyone, and she did the same. It was wonderful, and it really did promote closeness. There were no barriers or walls to hide behind; we trusted each other and felt comfortable in this openness.

One game we played was to tell what we each wanted in a mate or marriage. It was here that we both began to get answers about where our relationship should go. She wanted love, eventually children, and a musical career. I wanted love, affection, and companionship—and children were O.K., too. As we talked on, we realized that there was a potential conflict between her musical career and my need for companionship. The two could be incompatible. We talked in detail about the subject, then dropped it entirely as we both realized we were headed in different directions.

A few days later Patty returned to Oregon. We both were a little sad but recognized that we knew ourselves and each other better. There were no painful aches of the heart this time, but there was a genuine friendship that would last forever.

A year later Patty married her boyfriend.

For me, an important lesson had been learned. I had wasted a lot of pity on myself two years earlier. But I now realized that there would have been even more unhappiness and self-pity had I gotten my wishes then. I would have been terribly lonely while she spent her weekends and evenings pursuing her love of music and being a successful entertainer. Sometimes "the forces" know more than we do and act on our behalf, even when we think otherwise and try to resist the flow of events. I had temporarily forgotten how serendipity operates.

I wondered how many hours in my life I had spent in regret or dissatisfaction when I should have been thankful for the opportunities before me and used my time in making the most of them.

I thought, too, of how many of my married friends are less happy than I and envious of my freedom and independence. In fact, many of them have had one or more broken marriages. I realized also that marriage and family commitments might not have allowed me to relocate to Virginia Beach and work for the A.R.E., especially if my spouse hadn't shared my interest and enthusiasm for the Cayce work. Maybe I was meant to do other things than to be a husband and possible father in this lifetime. After all, I had many friends. I was, as the Cayce readings urge for everyone, content if not satisfied. I simply needed to put all my effort and time into the opportunities that were presently mine without the liabilities that go with regret and discontent.

CHAPTER SIXTEEN

On a Saturday morning in December of 1991, I received a phone call from Tom Weber. Tom now lived with his wife in Atlanta but was visiting his mother for the weekend in Louisville. He told me they had just heard on the radio that Tom Ballard had been murdered the night before. He didn't know any of the details but the address of my apartment building had been given.

I was stunned. All I could say over and over again was, "Oh, my goodness!"

It was several hours before I learned more. At first I was told that he had been beaten to death, but later I learned he had been mortally wounded in the head with a shotgun. The next day I talked to his brother, Charlie, who lived in an adjoining area of the building. Charlie told me that on Friday evening around 10:00 or 10:30, Tom had yelled Charlie's name, then a muffled explosion was heard. The door was locked between their two living areas, comprising my old apartment. He had to go around the building to enter Tom's unit from the rear door. This was the door Tom normally used to enter or leave his apartment. Tom was lying on the floor of the first room, his face a bloody mess, and he was obviously dead. There was no one else around, and Charlie called the police. A broken shotgun stock was found under Tom's body. Apparently there had been a brief struggle before Tom was shot.

It all sounded like a replay. The facts were eerily similar to the armed robbery and my shooting nearly eighteen years before. Robbery apparently was the motive again—his billfold had been taken—but there were no positive leads or suspects.

A memorial service was held a week later in a local church, and I was able to attend. (I had planned to be in Louisville then anyway on the way to my father's home in western Kentucky for the Christmas holidays.) Tom's body had been cremated—fulfillment of his oft-expressed desire—and the service was very moving and beautiful. The minister who spoke noted the incongruity of the whole thing: Forceful robbery and violence were totally unnecessary with Tom; he would give his last cent to anyone who appeared to need it. In fact, it may well have been this trait that resulted in his death. I had often wondered at the risk of his helping street bums and derelicts, simply because he saw that they were in need. To me they often appeared dangerous. Several stories were related about Tom's selfless generosity. I knew, probably better than anyone there, about this subject; I had been a major recipient of it.

The auditorium was filled, and I saw many old A.R.E. and study group friends, some of whom I hadn't seen in years. Tom's ashes were buried on the church grounds, and a reception with the family followed.

There were so many memories for me of turning points in my life in which Tom had played an important part. There were travels and trips, often with his two aunts. There were apartments we had remodeled or renovated, study group meetings, his hospital visits, his inestimable help in my recovery process, and his willingness to come to my aid, even traveling to Virginia Beach and beyond, whenever I needed it.

His death now by gunshot seemed to complete a cycle. Why were the events of his death so similar and reminiscent of my own shooting years before?

I remembered when he had first visited me in the hospital and said, "I wish it had been me they shot rather than you." Although he never said so, I think he felt somewhat guilty that I had been the one to bear the brunt and ill effects of the robbery and shooting in my home. He probably reasoned that he could have been more forceful in denying access to the intruders and that calling my name had brought me into their gunfire. But he didn't need to feel guilty. I, or anyone else, would probably have responded just as he had.

He also told me in the hospital that he had prayed and made a vow with God: If God would spare my life, he would take care of me until I was restored to health. He had certainly fulfilled his end of the bargain. Maybe he had now completed the tasks he was supposed to do in this life and had, therefore, been allowed to move on. While violent, his death had certainly been quick and, I presume, relatively painless.

I remembered the trip with Tom to Johns Hopkins Hospital when I was going for spinal implant surgery. We had listened in the car to a taped discussion by a man who had gone through a near-death experience. Although clinically dead for some time, the man had recovered to tell of his experiences and of the joy on the "other side." It was very moving and powerful. Tom asked for the tape and told me later he had listened to it many times.

In the spring of 1991, Tom had driven to Virginia Beach, and then the two of us had gone on to Atlanta for Tom Weber's wedding. Tom Weber had us sit with his family for the ceremony. For him, we each had been his surrogate father and friend. I saw Bill, his real father, for the first time since he had stopped by years before to ask that the study group look after Lynn. Somewhat emotionally he thanked Tom and me for fulfilling that request. He had no idea how we had been blessed in doing so.

On the return trip from Atlanta, Tom and I reminisced about the past and talked of life and death. He was still thoroughly grounded in the Cayce concepts about the continuity of life and the indestructibility of the soul. He said he had no fear of death and looked forward to the crossover. We, of course, couldn't know at the time that Tom would make the transition in just seven or eight months later. It was comforting now to know that he was ready for his pilgrimage when it arrived in the last month of 1991.

Maybe there was some symbolic promise in the fact that a new year lay just around the corner.

CHAPTER SEVENTEEN

Besides the death of Tom Ballard, the year 1991 had been difficult in other ways.

In the fall of 1990, the A.R.E. experienced financial problems, as did a lot of other organizations and individuals in the wake of a national economic downturn. It became obvious that some staff positions would have to be eliminated or curtailed if we were to hope to break even in 1991.

I felt relatively secure in my position as fund-raiser for the A.R.E.; it was an essential income area for supporting the service portions of our work. I was, therefore, quite surprised when Charles Thomas Cayce called me in and announced that my hours were to be reduced from forty to thirty weekly. I would have to get by on one-fourth less income.

This reduction in income could have been handled with minimum stress at one time. Actually, I had volunteered a few years before to take such a cut temporarily when the A.R.E. had gone through another tight financial period. But I had now purchased a condominium as my home, and I couldn't make ends meet with less income. I had some savings I could dip into, but this would last only so long.

As the significance of my situation sank in, I became disheartened and emotionally devastated. I had never experienced an arbitrary cut in pay before. Charles Thomas told me it shouldn't be construed as a demotion or dissatisfaction with my work but just one of a number of sacrifices required within the organization. There were good people who were terminated from employment, although some work areas seemed relatively unaffected. Nevertheless, I was in a personally difficult financial situation, and my mood was hardly helped by noting that at the end of the year my fund-raising department was the only one that showed an increase in income from the previous year.

My former boss at the Farm Credit Bank in Louisville once said, "I have always found that if you do your job well, the remuneration will take care of itself." I accepted his rationale and had always found it to be true. But now I wasn't so sure. Salaries at the A.R.E. had traditionally lagged behind comparable community standards, and that was understandable. But a quarter of mine was now gone without an apparent correlation to performance.

I had to make some hard decisions. Should I try to find employment elsewhere? Should I sell my home and rent something cheaper? Should I return to Kentucky? Had I made a mistake originally in coming to work at the A.R.E.?

A period of intense soul-searching was at hand. I prayed and meditated on the subject. I also watched my dreams for answers. None seemed to come, although there was probably significance in the fact that my dreams didn't indicate any impending major changes, nor presumably the need for them.

Maybe I had erred in purchasing my condominium home three years before. I had waited six years before making such a move and felt the time was right when I did so. I really looked at it as a sound long-term investment. I just hadn't anticipated a cut in my salaried income, from which mortgage payments had to come.

My commitment to the Cayce work and its ideals was as strong as ever. I felt, too, that I had something to offer the

A.R.E. with my job skills, and I wanted to continue in my present work and location.

Maybe it was time to review my spiritual ideals—the ones that the Cayce material had made so vivid and vital for me over the years.

First, I remembered the potent line in the "Patience" chapter of the study group's *A Search for God* book: "He that is without crosses has ceased to be of notice and is no longer among the sons [of God]." (p. 82) Just because I felt the A.R.E. work is God's work was no reason why my involvement with it should be exempt from crosses. Actually, the Cayce material suggests, so-called problems are opportunities in disguise.

But how would I pay my bills, at least after my savings were depleted?

Again I found answers in the Cayce readings—answers that Cayce had offered to people living in times much tougher than mine now, the Depression era and World War II.

> ... do not be afraid of giving self in a service—if the *ideal* is correct. If it is for selfish motives, for aggrandizement, for obtaining a hold to be used in an underhand manner, *beware*. If it is that the glory of truth may be made manifest, *spend it all*—whether self, mind, body, or the worldly means—whether in labor or in the coin of the realm. 1957-1

> For, know, the earth and all therein is the Lord's. The silver, the gold, the cattle on a thousand hills are His. He knows thy needs, but thou must *choose* as to what ye will do with the talents He hath given thee.
>
> As ye apply, as ye make use of that in hand, more is given thee. For, day unto day is sufficient, if use is made thereof... 1206-13

Based upon this advice, all I knew to do was just plod ahead, trusting that my material needs would be supplied. As I looked around me, others throughout the country were being tested in the economic arena as much or more than I.

What about serendipity—finding something valuable that wasn't sought? It suddenly dawned on me that I would have extra time to devote to a historical novel I had started and looked forward to finishing "some day." It was a pre-Revolutionary War story about legendary lost silver mines and a Virginian, John Swift, who reputedly found valuable silver in what is now eastern Kentucky before that area was settled. It would be great to complete that story—and I did so in the months that followed.

Conditions turned out to be not quite as tight financially as I had feared, but I did have to dip into my savings occasionally. Then a bomb hit. In August, my home air-conditioning and heating system went out; a major expenditure was required. What would I do if my car gave out also? I now had over 100,000 miles on it.

In retrospect, I think my faith was being tested just a little more. For just as suddenly, events took a turn for the better.

In September, I received an offer for the purchase of pulpwood from my tree farm in western Kentucky. I had borrowed money and purchased an old, worn-out farm during my last year in college. I had then set out trees, mostly pine, on the farm, but the necessary thinning of timber in later years had never been practical because of the absence of a market for pulpwood. The Westvaco Company had now moved into the county, and they wanted to buy trees for pulpwood. The cutting was a sound timber practice, and the income, although not great, turned out to be a little more than enough to pay for my new furnace and air conditioner.

A couple of months later I learned that my work hours would be restored by the beginning of the coming year.

There was a limit put on certain salary groupings, including mine, but I would now be working full-time and able to live within my financial means again.

Early in 1992 I realized it would be wise for me to refinance my home mortgage to take advantage of the lower interest rates now generally available. In the process of refinancing, I got a phone call from my father. He felt he was paying too much in income taxes and wondered if I could make use of a sum he was considering giving to my sister and me. Of course, the answer was affirmative, and this gift was applied to my mortgage. It reduced the monthly payments to a much more acceptable level.

I was beginning to believe in this "God will take care of you" stuff.

Then it really happened!

It was the last day of July, 1992—Friday the 31st, rather than Friday the 13th.

Catering to a recent sweet-tooth habit of eating pastries on the last workday of the week, I stopped at a Dunkin' Donuts® store on the way to work and purchased a couple of donuts and a cup of coffee. A contest was under way, and I accepted my game card with little thought and certainly no optimism. Upon arriving at my office ten minutes later, I munched on the breakfast at my desk. Then I remembered the contest, which required a matching of covered spots on the game card. All one had to do was pick three of the nine spots, rub off the covering to expose a dollar figure or prize underneath, and hope the three matched. I found a penny in my pocket and began rubbing off a couple of the nine covered spots. Much to my surprise, the two matched. I then read the rules further and realized that *three* spots had to match. Nonchalantly, I rubbed off the third. It read the same: $25,000!

There had to be some catch and, sure enough, there were some initials by each number. They were very small, and I wasn't sure if the initials were the same in all three spots. I got up, walked to the building entrance door, and grabbed Dee Sloan as she came in. She looked carefully at the card in the brighter outside light and excitedly stated, "Glenn, you've done it! You've won!" The small initials were the same in all three spots. I began to get a little excited myself, but still felt I must be overlooking something. I never win contests.

I called the local shop where I had made the purchase. The woman on the phone said something like, "Sure, and you have the Virginia lottery winning number, too, I guess." She warned me that I would have to pay taxes on anything I won. I guess she thought that bit of advice would silence me if I were just a dreamer or a crank. I insisted I really did have a winning $25,000 combination. She suggested that I bring the card in, and I told her I would be there in fifteen minutes.

When I arrived and announced my claim, the two women at the counter called the manager from the back. He looked at my ticket and then mild pandemonium broke out. He told me that the odds of winning the $25,000 top prize were forty-seven million to one and that there was only one such prize in the entire contest for this national chain. He called the regional manager and owner. A reporter was also called, and the resulting article in the local newspaper noted that these odds were nearly seven times as great as those for winning the state lottery. A few days afterward one of the local TV stations did a special news report on my good fortune.

When I got back to work that day, I found genuine excitement there, too. Needless to say, my own work productivity wasn't very great during the remainder of the day.

The rules required me to send my winning card to an address in Connecticut. I sent it that afternoon by registered, insured mail. Three weeks later, I still had received no official confirmation from the home office of having won. Doubts began to creep in. Was there some loophole to invalidate my card? The rules had said the card was void if there was an error in printing. Maybe there had been too many winning tickets printed, and they would deny my prize. Maybe they would claim a scratch on one of the unexposed circles voided the card. The rules stated that any partial removal of more than three spots would void the card. Although one spot did have a scratch, none of the printing underneath was exposed. I had no idea how the scratch had gotten there. Morally there should be no problem, but technically there conceivably could be.

Even though I tried to take the whole episode in stride and be low-key about it all, it was virtually impossible. Word of my fortune had spread rapidly, and I heard from some friends for the first time in years. It was a heady experience and fun, but what if I didn't really win? I remembered a few years before telling everyone about getting a return of feeling in my right leg, only to have it end shortly thereafter before there were any major results.

It began to seem like déjà vu. Was I again almost a winner but not quite? Was it just something to excite me and yet amount to nothing—like the healings that fizzled out or romantic encounters whose promise quickly vanished? If so, why? I would have been perfectly content had the card contained no identical spots as I had originally expected. But now it would be a bitter disappointment if the $25,000 weren't received. Maybe there was a lesson to be learned in this kind of "now you have it, now you don't" activity, but I couldn't recognize it.

It was also impossible, no matter how hard I tried, to avoid thinking about what I would do with the money if I received it. First, taxes would have to be paid on the prize. I wanted also to share this good fortune with the A.R.E by giving ten percent of the winnings to them. (I guess a fund-raiser who asks others to give also feels some responsibility to do the same.) Maybe I could use the remainder for traveling or other fun things. But then I saw others around me who obviously needed the money more than I. Maybe I should give some of it to them. There was no end to such needy causes. I began to appreciate a Cayce reading which cautioned a person who had inquired about how to get rich. In essence, Cayce's advice was to be careful about wanting to be in that situation in which he would continually have to say "yes" or "no" to those in great need:

> Are ye willing that such shall be thine *own* temptation? that ye are to build within thine experience that which will give thee, in thine own personal self, the right to say Yea and Nay to thy brother in want here and there? 826-9

Maybe this whole contest-winning episode had simply been an exercise to teach me the lesson of being satisfied with what I have without the dilemma of worrying about how to use any excess. I talked to some friends about the issue of being sensitive to those who seemed to be in greater need than I. They suggested that the universe works with meaning and purpose, that the win had come to me, and that it was intended for my use. At least I would tithe ten percent to the A.R.E., and I decided to follow my inner guidance and pay particular attention to my dreams on use of the remainder. I couldn't help but note that I would have enough to pay for the new car that had so concerned me when things were tight the year before. Above all, however, I wished something definitive would happen to let me know if I was going to get the money; the delay and uncertainty were difficult.

Finally I received official confirmation that I had won the $25,000. The check arrived a couple of weeks later, along with a photographed delivery ceremony at the store where the purchase had been made.

Maybe the cycle of near misses was finally broken. I discovered a Cayce reading which for me said it all:

And when ye trust in Him, ye are sure—and need never be afraid of the material things. For, does He not feed the birds of the air? Does He not give the color to the lily, the incense to the violet? How much more is that as may be in His very presence, if ye apply self to become worthy of acceptance in His home.   3333-1

I realized that I was extremely lucky and had been specially blessed. For me, it was corroboration that I should continue to try to do what I felt was right, and the other concerns such as my material needs would be supplied—maybe even with a little bounty. It was a lesson whose value in the long run might be worth far more than $25,000.

CHAPTER EIGHTEEN

When I began working at the A.R.E., Charles Thomas Cayce had gratuitously promised, "We're going to get you healed and married."

Neither one had quite happened.

At the time that I started getting some new healing and a return of feeling in my paralyzed right leg, I began writing about the events that had occurred to me since being shot. I was sure then that the healing would be total and that my pain would soon be over. I had planned to conclude the story with that climactic event. But it had never happened.

I felt that, unless I had some kind of miraculous healing and recovery, there was no finished story to tell. Without significant relief from my paralysis and leg pains, there was no need to complete the narrative I had started. So the writing project was put aside.

Of course, there had been many miracles along the path. The way my life was spared and the fact that I had recovered far beyond the predictions of my doctors were both amazing developments. I had experienced and witnessed firsthand the operations of serendipity and synchronicity. I had found that I could truly get guidance from my intuition and dreams, and I had discovered the value—actually the necessity—of accepting the events of life by flowing with them rather than wasting time in looking backward in pity and regret. I had been blessed materially in many ways—even at forty-seven million to one odds.

There had also been other blessings for which I was genuinely thankful. I had often looked back and realized how fortunate I was in leaving the Farm Credit Bank when I did. Depressed agricultural prices had triggered economic havoc in the farm credit business. Many loans couldn't be repaid, and mortgage foreclosures had become common. The Bank and many of its associations had experienced capital problems resulting in reorganizations and consolidations. It had been a very turbulent time in which several successor presidents of my bank had been replaced. I had been spared all this agony.

In addition, although at times it was barely perceptible, my physical condition had improved slightly each year. The prophecy of Dr. Leichtman really seemed to be coming true.

I had much to be thankful for, yet where was the healing to end my long night of the soul? I had a generally positive attitude most of the time, but occasionally doubt and frustration creeped in and seemed warranted.

Then I remembered a story which I heard or read years ago. It was called "The Promised Land" and went something like this:

Jim and Kate had grown up near each other on farms in western New York. They both had come from poor tenant families, and when they married they decided to leave New York and search for the promised land. They heard it was on the flat, fertile plains of Illinois.

So they moved there to prosper and start their home. The first year went fairly well; they broke even financially. But a severe drought wiped out all their crops the next year. They heard about another promised land—Kansas—and moved on.

Kansas was not quite what they expected either. The wind blew and howled all year long, carrying snow in the winter and soil and dust in the summer. They realized that this wasn't their dream and after a few years moved to Nebraska.

Events didn't go too well there the first couple of years, but they were surely set for big things thereafter, with an early spring plowing and planting in the third year. A prairie fire in August, however, destroyed not only their crops but their home as well. In the small town nearby, a passing stranger told Jim about gold strikes in Colorado. This had to be the promised land, and so they packed the family and possessions and headed for the gold fields to strike it rich.

But the "hot" spots had already been found in the gold and silver mines, and there were no quick fortunes to be made. Jim was able, however, to eke out enough money for the family to survive by working at odd jobs for a couple of years.

And so it went. The promised land was always just around the corner, even when they supposedly had arrived there.

From Colorado, they went to the promised lands of Montana, then Arizona, Nevada, and finally California. But not even California turned out to be their long-sought-after goal. By then Jim, now nearly sixty, died of a heart attack.

It was some months later that Kate began thinking of the past—of youthful and better days. They had raised a family—three boys and two girls—who all now had children of their own. They had never gotten rich in terms of money, but Kate was rich with memories. They had been happy through all of those years that at the time seemed to be difficult.

Almost too late Kate realized she had been in the promised land all along. She only wished Jim had made this discovery before he left her, but she knew that he, too, had been happy. And, come to think of it, he hadn't brought up the subject of the promised land for several years. They had been blessed with their love for each other and with many pleasures of life—all treasures that a promised land, no matter how bountiful, couldn't have surpassed.

The promised land, she recognized, was not a place but a state of mind—one of contentedness, love, and enjoyment of the good things in life that come one's way.

Remembering that story, I now realized that my promised land—the healing I had sought after for so long—was really less important than what was already mine. Sure, I had pain that put some limits on my enjoyment of life, but there were so many good things I did have that I actually had been in El Dorado all along and hadn't recognized it. Some of the blessings that were most important to me might not have come my way if I had received the healing that had been my primary goal and obsession through the years.

My friends, job, home, and all other possessions were the product of the life path I had followed. Had it been changed in any significant way, these blessings might not now be mine. They are more important to me than the end to my pain and paralysis. This, in itself, had been serendipity in operation through the years. Pursuing what I thought to be a promised land of physical healing, I had truly found even more valuable treasures.

Now I understand from the depths of my being—out of long personal experience—these words of a Cayce reading:

Count it rather as an opportunity, a gift of a merciful Father, that there *are* the opportunities in the present for the sojourn in the material influences; that the advantages may be taken of opportunities that come into the experience, even through the hardships and disappointments that have arisen.   1709-3

In joy and gratitude, I thus thank the Creator and God of

us all for every joy and blessing which has enriched and enlightened my life and for the treasures which have brightened and illuminated the night, even when I almost failed to notice. I realize now that the night for some time has been shining as though in the light of day. At long last for me and without surrendering an attitude of expectancy and hope, the darkness and the night shall be no more.

Yea, the darkness hideth not from thee, but the night shineth as the day: the darkness and the light are both alike to thee.   Psalm 139:12, KJV

APPENDIX A

The following is a psychic reading given by Al Miner and discussed in Chapter Eleven. It was requested after an earlier reading from him which touched upon past lives I reputedly had experienced. I had been particularly intrigued about a claimed past life in which I was part of an early Christian "Council of Constantine." Answers about this Council and to questions about other possible past lives, as well as my beginning work at the A.R.E., are parts of this reading.

ETA FOUNDATION
PSYCHIC READING for
GLENN SANDERFUR
By Al Miner
(August 19, 1982)

LUCY MINER: Our Father, who art in heaven, hallowed be Thy name. Thy kingdom come, Thy will be done on earth, as it is in heaven. Give us this day our daily bread and forgive us our debts, as we forgive our debtors, and lead us not into temptation but deliver us from evil. For Thine is the kingdom and the power and the glory forever and ever.

Dear Father/Mother/God, again we ask Thy blessings on this gathering. We ask Thy continued strength, guidance, and protection be placed on the channel and myself, although serving on your planes and these and all mankind. And we ask very special prayers, love, guidance, and blessings on the entity we are about to serve. We ask this in Thy name, Father, full well knowing if it be Thy will, then so shall it be done. We thank Thee, Father. Amen.

You are now at that level that is best suited for this reading. AL MINER speaking through the source identified as LAMA SENG: Yes, we are present, we ask the blessings of the Master to be with each of thee as well.

LUCY: Thank you, Lama Seng, and thank you once again for coming forward to join us this evening. This is August 19, 1982. Edward Glenn Sanderfur. Address is . . . Born January 22, 1934. Code # 1959.

LAMA SENG: Yes, we have references which apply to the entity now present. We have seen these in the past.

LUCY: Yes, we have, Lama Seng. He writes: "A previous reading indicated that I participated in a former life in the Council of Constantine and was excommunicated from it. Was this Council at Nicaea and can you supply more details as to my name, home country, and what I did as a consequence of this banishment? What is the significance of that life to this one?"

[From previous reading: "Later we find you present at a time when the teachings of a man called Jesus were being discussed and the stories which were written about Him and His works were being reviewed. You were a literary scholar recognized for your ability to translate dialect in various languages. Commissioned by one of great power, a king, to sit upon this Council, you became so engrossed, so captivated with the teachings, thus, it led to your loss of position. You were banished, but not to any concern to you, for you returned and followed and traced the heritage of this story and learned very much—a very beautiful lifetime. Here again, then, find within self that those things which impose themselves upon your true joy need not be heeded to the extent that they cloud the seeking, joyful wonder, and awe which exists within you. The last purpose, then, to fulfill a thirst, a desire for knowledge, to inspire the creative source of that knowledge and to, in a way, give this as a living example to others. You may write of this, you may tell of it, you may live it, that is your choice, see?" (The reading later referred to this Council as the Council of Constantine.)]

LAMA SENG: This is that Council wherein there was the decision to make this whole doctrine be clear in those words which were to be carried forward and those judgments as related to matters of church and state. And those who had power or authority tended to wield same over those who were the scholars, the seers, and the interpreters. And in this Council there were several whose voices were heard here at Nicaea and here at the other meeting places, as well, who spoke of certain methodologies, teachings, certain works needed to be preserved or persevered in their more literal translation. There was strong opposition to this and opposement to many forms of teaching which had evolved from these translations. This became not only a spiritual work, but a highly political and one which involved many levels of man's consciousness or ego, as well.

Hence, there were great struggles. These evolved to a point where certain of these entities who opposed the greater masses, who were swayed by the authority and the promise of power, thusly were excommunicated, in a manner of speaking, or purged from the Council. This did not dampen nor refute the belief of you and several of the others, and you formulated a grouping of peoples who sought to persevere with these works. There was the movement then, throughout different times, one of which became a temple or a shrine for certain of these teachings called

"Mount Athos." There was the movement into the Greek into different lands and into those areas which became to be founded as the purveyors of truth and the teachers of the philosophical as well as the literal meaning of the works or writing. There was the movement of some of these into the lands of the Anglican and others into the lands of the Celts. We find the works which you perpetuated thereafter were those which were continually opposed and ultimately there was the manipulation which caused you, as an outcome or result, your life.

The parallel to the present is the seeking and bringing forth of truth, and though this be not that Council again, there are certain of those entities who were present in that incarnation who can again be found present in your current incarnation with you. We find that these, some of them, come and go, many of them in fact, and some of them, a handful, reside in your locale with you, but not all are involved in this work directly. Others are involved in other locales and in other ways. The purpose for the giving of this comment to you in past is to acquaint you in the present that truth cannot be suppressed. That it will continue to emerge and to be brought forward and that the works as given by the entity called "Edgar" are some signets of this that we have just spoken. Wherein his, as a work, lie before mankind, they can be accepted or rejected by the choice of the individual and by the groups. And yet, they endure, even with the affronting to have, at times, cast upon others who have sought to maintain their rule, their dogma, their teaching.

LUCY: I was going to ask that question: "Does he know any of them in his involvement with A.R.E. at this point?" But you've answered that also. Can you give Glenn name, home country, if this is possible or allowed at this time?

LAMA SENG: I might call him a Byzantinian.

LUCY: Anything more?

LAMA SENG: The name which is given as Marius or Maris, see?

LUCY: O.K., anything further on that incarnation, Lama Seng, that would be interesting or helpful for Glenn to know at this point?

LAMA SENG: There were many others who sought power. A gathering of small groupings and by the bringing together of support or supporters, sought to bring forth their interpretation and their will and their decisions as to the pathway that certain religious matters would follow and that certain teachings would be, as such, interpreted as. We would find that yours was in those times, some of those who had come forward through several incarnations with thee, even as you would find some of those have come into this incarnation with thee, in the present. Yours was the crest in that time, which largely carried the shield of the Eastern churches and those which carried the orthodoxy as its tenant, a literal translation. Here we would find in the current incarnation there is the interpretive, rather than the literal; the implied and the spirit as it is borne by the entire book and statement, rather than just a word here and there. It is to this reason that you find yourself so often struggling with just a word, just a passage, just a phrase as can be given in His works, or the Master's directive, see?

LUCY: "Did I have a previous incarnation at or about the time of Jesus?"

LAMA SENG: Yes.

LUCY: O.K. "Did I know any of the disciples, and, if so, do I know them in this lifetime and what is the significance of that now if I did?"

LAMA SENG: Yes, there was knowledge of same in those times and some of them in the present. Significant is the fact that your return and their influence are combined to meet the presence of the Master's Spirit in the earth. The significance is the preparation of the earth and of mankind to receive His presence. Each should seek to open self, for the change will be made manifest within the individual first and then spread to the groups and to the peoples or countries or lands. And then, prayerfully and joyously, we would pray that there would be the presence of that light on the entirety of the earth, see?

LUCY: Lama Seng, will you tell him more at this time about his incarnation at or about the time of Jesus?

LAMA SENG: Too much dealing in this regard at this time will mislead or cause the entity to focus too intently upon the past.

LUCY: O.K. Do you want to state anything more on that question then at this point, or I'll move forward?

LAMA SENG: There was the knowledge of one of these who is now in these realms, and who has left his mark, his work, for others to follow, and whose influence may, if he chooses, return, as he would choose, and as the Master would have his presence in His works. We would find that there are other influences that are known and that may be experienced in these same veins.

Those times when the Master's presence was upon the earth were very active times for all of those who were seeking and who had prepared by way of their incarnated processes and those who had, by way of their group works, developed and brought to the fruition those energies and those levels of consciousness so as could provide a nucleus or nuclei for those teachings to be builded sort of as one would prepare a ground to receive its seed. And so, we find, that the teachings that you learned in those times were those which you sought to record very diligently and those which you sought to share and discussed at great length with others, such as Nicodemus and others, who spoke with wisdom and spoke with authority. See?

LUCY: O.K. "Please give any further information or advice concerning this life or past lives which would be important to me now and aid in my spiritual development."

LAMA SENG: In the current, dear friend, all of your past experiences are being stimulated. What we are attempting to convey to you is that all of the sum total of your being has an energy passing through it, so that collectively, these are focusing just as a broad sphere might be focused by a ray of light or projected onto a certain location, a certain spot, if you will. We find that in the present, energies from the Persian, from the Greek, from the Atlantean, from those times in the lands of Israel, from the Egyptian, from South America and from numerous other lands upon which you have walked in varying forms, in varying bodies, in different races of man and in different thought forms, it is the sum, or the collective of self, which now is focused in the present. Why? Because yours is the position, yours is the opportunity, to truly in this lifetime know self, and thus, by the understanding of self and the influences which have gone before the reactions from same, ye can build an image which can be an example for others and which can help to bring forth that light once again, just as it did in the past.

In the lands of Israel, yours was a position of authority and freedom, being free-born and in a station of some wealth. You were not touched by those who came as the Romans because of your status and because of your national heritage and extraction. You were considered to be a very wise entity and you were consulted often in matters of law and protocol and physics and medicine. You became known somewhat for your clear thinking and for your ability to decide difficulties, even though they were close to the heart. You were generally known as "the Greek," but you were not purely Greek, for your mother was of a far-distant land, but as such, you inherited the righteousness and the authority that was respected by their scholars and by their teachers. When you, at a very early age, entered this land to claim that which was your inheritance, you did so in a manner which was well received by these people and not in the normal sense as an outsider might have been.

So you became, then, involved with works of literary nature and became involved later with the recording of certain teachings which were brought to the fore by the Carpenter, and you were then, later, to learn of His travels and become enthralled with them, meeting with several whom you highly respected who were then seers of the Essenic environ. You were guided by these and others to meet with certain of His representatives and there was a good union here and many works followed. We are not permitted to go beyond these. The reason this is important for you in the present is because you have evolved in a manner of a cyclic pattern to the present time once again. You will recall some of those comments we have given to you humbly in past, and, if you combine those with that as has been given here, it should provide you with a clear perspective of that which has gone before. Understanding this, then, do not dwell upon it or reconstruct that image, but draw from it to create the better image of the present. See?

LUCY: We will move forward. "How can I make my work at the A.R.E. more effective? Is my best use there in the Office of Development?"

LAMA SENG: For the present, this is a very important use of your talents or abilities. But not just in an office, but in the attitude which you bring to these peoples. The enthusiasm and the clarity of purpose and mind help them to see themselves as a reservoir of truth and let this be persevered in above all. You will be asked to fill other capacities and very soon, if not even at the present, when you hear these words on this device, but consider that it isn't the work as much as it is the attitude with which you proceed. See?

LUCY: O.K. "Please give a curent evaluation of the work of the A.R.E. How can the A.R.E. better fulfill its purpose of 'making manifest the love of God and man'? What changes, if any, should be made?"

LAMA SENG: Father, as we seek to respond to this inquiry now before us, we pray of Thee that we be permitted to do so in deepest humility and love. We ask that we be permitted, in accordance with the will of Thy presence and in honor, always to those works which have gone before and which shall follow. We thank Thee in humbleness, Father, and with joy. Amen.

LUCY: Amen.

LAMA SENG: Just as one would find that each traveler needs nourishment and looks for, longs for, refreshment of the body, the mind, the body, and the spirit, even though they know only the relationship of body and mind, many of them, when truth is heard or felt or experienced, it will open and awaken certain aspects of their being and bring them light. It is not for [us] here, as humble servants of our Father, to state to thee that thou must do this and that, but rather that each would seek to be the better guided by the forces of God and let these bring selves unto that labor which is performed joyously and in unison. What is needed in the earth is truth and light, not so much so that an entity is overwhelmed by same, but in a sense of an offering, as one would extend a cup of water to a weary traveler. It is not forced upon them; it is extended in graciousness and in loving compassion. Thus, do not be forbearing but be, rather, receptive and loving. Be cautious so as to not fall too deeply into the image of the earth, but rather stand apart from it as a light would stand apart from darkness. Be the example, each of you, in your ways, in your attitudes and in your works of that which you seek to preserve, for it is written that man is judged by that which he holds in his heart and mind, more so than by that which he holds in his hand.

It is also important that there be a review again of the directions and the works for each entity that each can be given to the greater ability of their talent—that which is theirs to perform joyfully. A review again of the overall desires of those who control and protect, for these must be in accord with the works and what the works have stated to be the purpose and future for their existence. Again, we state these are comments given in complete humbleness and not in a sense of authority, but as a companion would guide and speak to a fellow. See?

LUCY: Very well, Lama Seng, any further comments there or on any other questions that Glenn has asked at this point or anything you would like to state from your vantage point? Physical, mental, spiritual?

LAMA SENG: It will be well for all of you to review among yourselves, collectively and as individuals, your visions and dreams during these and the forthcoming times, for as surely as these are His works, then shall He guide thee as individuals and as a grouping. These works must stand out. These works must endure, and they must be made available to those who will seek them. We use these words of strength because they are given to [us] here, and as we believe in them, it is our prayer that ye shall also find in them strength. Ofttimes, we do not know fully our Father's will in terms of the why this or that is given, and we know that in the earth this can be a matter of some concern and also frustration. Hear and then apply the faith to feel the knowledge of wisdom behind these and let it flow with thee. See?

LUCY: Very well, Lama Seng. Unless you have anything further you would like to discuss with Glenn, we will thank you very, very much.

LAMA SENG: More comment will be given in those times ahead. For the present, much of what is given is limited, to an extent, because of the need of growth of the individuals who are involved. As the result of those activities which are perpetuated in these works at present, many entities will find opportunity of growth and evolvement and that is a portion of the purpose of these works of Edgar and these works as given here.

Let each entity seeking be given the opportunity of finding that which is their growth. Have a good cheer and a glad heart, for your pathway is surely aright. Fear not, but go forward in gladness. We have been most humble and, indeed, joyous to have been with thee once again. Know, ever, that our prayers and our blessings in our Father's name are ever with thee. For the present, we must conclude. Fare the well, dear friends.

LUCY: Fare thee well, Lama Seng. Thank you, and you may release the channel at this time.

APPENDIX B

The following psychic reading is discussed in Chapter Twelve and was requested for purposes of current information and comparison with earlier psychic readings from Al Miner.

LIFE READING 842061 for
GLENN SANDERFUR
By Anne Puryear
(Given at Phoenix, Arizona, on August 18, 1984)

[Opening prayer by Herbert B. Puryear (HBP).]

Anne Puryear (AP): As we have here the pattern, the soul, the body, mind, and spirit, the following will be given to him:

There is that in the way of a cross of light from the head to the feet, covering the entire body of this one. For he has come in this lifetime for a special mission. And through the radiating of the Christ light through him, he will touch the lives of many souls who are struggling. And through the sharing of that light, help to bring tools for transformation through that which he has overcome and bring hope to those who have lost hope. As we find him here now on the pathway, it will be given to him in this way with help of the guardian and the eternal angel assigned to him.

This one chose the time and the place of his birth for the strengths that would be needed for this age to serve. And to learn particular lessons through the early childhood experiences and through the life that would enable him this lifetime to use the full resources available within him. To do that in the way to bring a ministry to those without a sense of hope. Therefore, now let the questions of his heart be asked.

HBP: Yes, please give a full and specific statement of Glenn's soul purpose for this incarnation, his life purpose, and goal.

AP: This one has come in this lifetime to recognize his strengths from the past lifetimes, and in the recognizing of these, to see himself as the Creator sees him. In so doing, then, take this awareness of the many sojourns in the physical body upon this earthly plane and use that awareness to strengthen the pattern [in] this lifetime so that he might accomplish that which he covenanted to do before taking this physical body. He has come in to work with the laws of healing, both physical and spiritual. He has come in also to learn to use the awareness within him to reach out past himself and share that with others. This one has come to serve through his communications and has the greater part of his life purpose yet ahead, for his true ministry has not yet begun.

HBP: And may some of the nature of that ministry be given or is it in that he is to work in the manner just given in terms of the soul purpose?

AP: He has come in with that in the way of the symbol in the auric field of the golden book beginning to open. This one has come to write about his experiences and to bring light and hope and help to those through the sharing of that which has occurred through his life. That which will occur as he allows himself to heal totally and go on with his life in new directions and, through the sharing of this, touch the masses. He has come in also to learn to use the voice in the verbal communication to such an extent that there can be healing through the voice and again in future years to touch the lives of many through such sharing. He has also come to search out, to understand that which will heal the body, mind, and spirit, and, in so healing himself, share those tools with others and bring help to those who know not where to search, who know not the direction in whence to go.

HBP: Please give the incarnations of this entity in the earth plane in which there has been the greater spiritual work—those incarnations having a greater effect on the present incarnation, especially with respect to the soul purpose.

AP: As we have here the records, the following will be given: This is another of the old souls returning upon the planet at this time. During a time of much change, of much chaos and darkness and difficulty, to be a light bearer for this new age. To make a difference, that through the changes within himself, truly this will radiate out to others and bring hope in the despair. So has chosen this time period for a purpose.

He began the incarnating experiences during the Lemurian times. And throughout that which greatly paralleled the Atlantean times, of which little is written. It would be most important for this one to work with the meditations or the hypnosis or the inspirational writing in such a way as to release much that has seemingly been hidden from these times. That will bring help to mankind at this time in history. In the Lemurian times there was an awareness and an ability to freely communicate and walk between dimensions. There was that in the way of the spiritual attunement and walking in the oneness and in light. Also in that time, there was knowing of the continuity of life and not the fear of death or birth into the physical.

He then became one who chose to make a series of incarnations into the Atlantean period and in so doing this one during the three periods in Atlantis was actively involved as a student and as a teacher. And in the second of the Atlantean periods, this was one who traveled throughout the land as one who might be called a judge or one who went to many circuits to bring the greater guidance and the keeping of the law. And as he went to many places, he was known throughout the land as one who had the great wisdom to make of those things that were given the kinder, the greater, choices. In so doing, much growth that lifetime, but there was not the strong awareness of the use of the intuitive in the second period; therefore, he became a student in the schools of light during that time for several incarnations and learned much in working with the intuitive and the higher awareness. In so doing, then came back as a male after four incarnations to work again with helping those keep the laws of the land to prepare for the better peace and awareness, for there was the knowing by many who had the awareness that if there were not the changes made in the technology and the misuse of nature at the time that there would occur again a destruction of a more severe nature than that which had already occurred.

In going throughout the land to help with working of the keeping of the law and peace, there was much good done. But much also fell upon deaf ears. And there was the continuing by many of that which would ultimately cause the second destruction or the breaking up into the islands and that which was truly of the more difficult time than even the third destruction. For at that time of the second period, there was such difficulty and loss of lives that it was hundreds of years before there was the recuperating from this by many; neverthless, he was one who tried to bring light in such. He was in physical body during the second destruction where there was the breaking into the islands, and he took a band of those to a place of safety. And they worked with helping to rebuild.

He did not come back for several hundred years into the third period. Then when he did, he came back as one who was an instructor in the schools of light, greatly changed from that time, and did that in the way of the preparing of the students, both old and young, in the way of that which he taught and planned and organized, so that these would be trained to be the leaders. In so doing then, this one was a part of that experience of the 200 years of peace in the third Atlantean period and was known to selves in that period and many others. And during that time, helping to keep the peace upon the land and bringing of the greater joy. There was then the pulling away from that by many, but always this one had the greater peacefulness of nature throughout the Atlantean sojourns.

He was not in physical form during that which was the third destruction where most of the land of the Atlantean went beneath the water, but rather was in the spiritual realm helping across those souls who made the transition by the thousands during that time. There will be in his lifetime, the revealing of records in three places that will prove and bring greater credibility, not only to the Edgar Cayce readings about Atlantis, but to that which is the feeling within the hearts of many of the old Atlanteans, such as himself, that will bring a verification of feelings that have been long hidden about this particular time period.

This was one in the Egyptian place who was a follower into exile of he who was Ra Ta. Therefore, it is part of that which creates the loyalty or the going into the working with the records of this one who then became a channel of light in other lifetimes. So a part of this comes from that time period and was for many years in exile strongly supporting this one, not always agreeing with some of those things, but a strong supporter.

He then began a series of incarnating experiences in Egypt that had him a part of that which was the group that would later have some of the truth and information brought to that which was the Essene community many hundreds of years afterwards. In so doing, was one who first learned at the feet of many of the masters in the upper and lower Egyptian places in many lifetimes both male and female, even to working with that in the way of the movement of the body through that which would be called the dance, and also the use of the voice in the chanting or the toning or the singing, to help elevate the consciousness. He also was one who worked with the stringed instrument and using of the instrument to raise the vibrations within the physical body. A part of what he learned in the mystery school, so to speak, in the Egyptian time, can be helpful through the remembering and the inner listening to be brought to this life pattern for that which will ultimately be a total healing of the soul.

In the Egyptian place also, he was a part of a secret society in a female body that had that which was worn around the neck to give them admittance to those places where there were the secret teachings. For the teachings were of a strength that had they been used by the normal people of the time, could have been misused. So there was the meeting in secret and working with the energies of levitation, dematerialization, and those things of passing objects through objects in order to help in the building and strengthening of the time. The books by Joan Grant, *Lord of the Horizon, Winged Pharaoh, Many Lifetimes,* and others, would be helpful to him in the understanding of that which he himself experienced, both male and female, during those time periods. For this one, as is given by she who is Joan Grant, even had at one time a lion as a pet. We find him in other Egyptian periods and especially during that which was the time where the Great Pyramid was used as a temple of initiation. And in that, the soul still carries in the cells of the body the remembrance of these times.

We find him, too, in the period throughout Palestine, and in so understanding this, many of the sojourns of service during that time were to help him have the greater understanding of those who would be the people of the time. He from the land throughout many places in one of the experiences in a male body in a nomadic tribe, going to these many places and learning much. It was not a lifetime of great growth but of taking in much information that would be used in the future. Then in and around the area in Palestine, close to that of the area where many of the high energies still exist, this was one of those who was a part of the Essene community, making for the preparation in three lifetimes for that which would be the preparation of the entrance of the Master. He was in physical form during the birth of He who walked the land and made it holy and was known to Him and to the family and served Him loyally and faithfully during the years. Was not present at the crucifixion but was present during that which was the time after and those years of taking forward the truth. And this one was well known to he who was Paul during that time, and a supporter of this one, though the two not always agreeing, the strong support and the taking forward of the teachings. This is a part of one who made the covenant or the covenanting group of one who came not from this place but from the Arcturian energies, and it would do him well to study not only this but also the inner attunement to bring him much guidance.

This is also an old Hopi, an Apache, a Commanche, and many of the Indian tribes that would be known and some not known to him from the past. For, through walking with these many in these tribes, both warring and peace, there was much that was learned by him that has brought him to this time period.

This lifetime being a culmination of these past experiences to this extent. If he accomplishes [in] this lifetime that which he came in to do, he may well desire not to return again in physical form. But if he does return it will be in pure service in the years ahead after much change. During his experience as a part of the Hopi tribe, this one worked with a strong healing ability, not only an ability to heal himself, but to direct energies through him to those who came seeking. In so doing, many of the things used by the Hopi, which were similar to those things of the Kahuna, are those healing techniques that can be used this lifetime to restore the body, the mind, the spirit to the oneness needed for the work in the years yet ahead.

This one, because of the karma brought in from past lifetimes of a positive nature, has the ability to do two things this lifetime: One, to extend the life pattern many years in order to serve most effectively in the later years, and also to create through his own endeavors and communications, that in the way of abundance and supply, not only to free him in the future to do more of the life's work, but to share with others. These are the promises. He simply has but to reach his arms to the heaven and ask and that which he asks will be poured out upon him if he will ask believing, trusting, and act upon that which is given to him. These are but a few of literally hundreds and hundreds of lifetimes of this old soul of light, for there is not a place upon this planet that he has not been.

HBP: Glenn asks, "What was the significance of my being shot on January 8, 1974, and being left with partial paralysis and severe leg pains: Are the paralysis and pains necessary for the rest of my life?"

AP: As there is the bringing forth of these records, it will be given in this way: This is most unusual in that this one is not repaying that which he has done in the past to another. This one has not come in in such a way as to be reaping that which he has sown. But this one came in taking upon him that which is an opportunity for great soul growth in one lifetime. Therefore, that which occurred was no accident, but there was an opportunity for that one which inflicted the damage to make of the different choices and through allowing himself to be one who would experience this if the correct choices were not made. He came in with the strength to bring total healing to the body in such a way as to stand as a light bearer to those who have lost hope, who have stumbled in the darkness, who are in despair. He has the ability through his own awareness and listening to be worked with by the angels, his guides and guardians, to such an extent that he can totally restore the body, alleviate the pain completely, and through the restoration, his life, his changes, his awareness, be that which brings help to many hundreds of people. He has chosen to come in to experience this to overcome, to heal for the greater growth. It is not a task that many would take upon them, but it is that which he himself has shouldered for this growth.

* * *

HBP: These are all the questions at this time. Glenn says, "I would appreciate any other advice or direction that would be helpful to me now."
AP: To let him know that during the lifetime that he walked with the Master, that not only the Master, but a group of those worked with helping to heal those who would come for the restoration of sight, for the restoration of the limbs, and for many other things that had occurred at the time—sometimes of long duration, many, many years. In so knowing this, that the same things that He, Jesus, was taught, so, too, was he himself taught. It will be helpful for him in his inspirational listening and writing to ask regarding those particular methods, and information will be given

to him. If he will also understand of his ability to communicate directly with God, that it is not that reserved for a few nor need it be that outstanding experience where the room is filled with light and there is the overpowering feeling of the Spirit, but rather more often, it is as walking with Him day by day along the pathway and asking and He will speak directly and guide. And sometimes He sends the angels and the guides to work with him. He is involved at this time within an organization where his light can radiate out from him and be effective in healing and balancing many energies that are disrupted. In so knowing this, he has chosen to come to experience this for a period of time to be one who brings the peace and harmony where there is not.

Also to know that he who was in the physical body, Edgar Cayce, having had many past lifetimes in service, has not finished that which is the work and desires to speak in and through many that truly have a desire and dedication to continue that work. Therefore, it is not the imagination that there will be times when this one will desire also to bring much in the way of information and help. There are those who have died that in no way have their progress slowed by communicating with them for they are a sign for periods of time to help those still caught in the denser earthly energies. But it is most important for him at this time to recognize that which is the power of the angelic forces working with him; in so doing, to use this power for they will not work unasked except for the three assigned to him. Therefore, in times of stress and difficulty, can call in not only angels of healing but angels of inspiration, and understanding the many levels of these, can use this great power for healing, for greater attunement, and enlightenment. It is also a time for him to begin to trust the intuitive and to use the intuitive combined with the intellect in the making of the decisions and the changing of the life in the healing process. As he begins to know himself as he is known, it can usher in for him the time of greatest joy, the time of greatest service, but also it is a time to activate courage and strengths—to touch the lives of those who stumble at this time in the darkness. He has much strength and ability to use the higher mind in the visualization, but it must be that as a muscle is stretched—practice and practice—until there is the greater strength of the using of this ability of the mind, the higher awareness.

One moment. This will also be given: The room at this time is filled with the presences of those who work with him and who desire to make their presence known to him. Therefore, as he listens to that, so, too, will there be feeling of those in the room with him; let him trust and sense that and act upon that, and in so doing, the light will flow in and through him and radiate out to many. Many of the things that he has done this lifetime, he has done in the past, but many of the things he has done in the past, he is not yet fully aware of in this lifetime. It is through the combining of this knowledge, both the past and the present, that he truly will build that which will be a light to the world. These things given to him sealed upon him in light. So be it.

[At the conclusion of the reading, Glenn was identified as belonging to a particular soul grouping of twenty-four persons. Glenn was encouraged to get in touch with the contact person for the group. His name was Brad, the same person mentioned in the text whom psychic Al Miner earlier had told to contact Glenn.]

What Is A.R.E.?

The Association for Research and Enlightenment, Inc. (A.R.E.®), is the international headquarters for the work of Edgar Cayce (1877-1945), who is considered the best-documented psychic of the twentieth century. Founded in 1931, the A.R.E. consists of a community of people from all walks of life and spiritual traditions, who have found meaningful and life-transformative insights from the readings of Edgar Cayce.

Although A.R.E. headquarters is located in Virginia Beach, Virginia—where visitors are always welcome—the A.R.E. community is a global network of individuals who offer conferences, educational activities, and fellowship around the world. People of every age are invited to participate in programs that focus on such topics as holistic health, dreams, reincarnation, ESP, the power of the mind, meditation, and personal spirituality.

In addition to study groups and various activities, the A.R.E. offers membership benefits and services, a bimonthly magazine, a newsletter, extracts from the Cayce readings, conferences, international tours, a massage school curriculum, an impressive volunteer network, a retreat-type camp for children and adults, and A.R.E. contacts around the world. A.R.E. also maintains an affiliation with Atlantic University, which offers a master's degree program in Transpersonal Studies.

For additional information about A.R.E. activities hosted near you, please contact:

> A.R.E.
> 67th St. and Atlantic Ave.
> P.O. Box 595
> Virginia Beach, VA 23451-0595
> (804) 428-3588

A.R.E. Press

A.R.E. Press is a publisher and distributor of books, audiotapes, and videos that offer guidance for a more fulfilling life. Our products are based on, or are compatible with, the concepts in the psychic readings of Edgar Cayce.

We especially seek to create products which carry forward the inspirational story of individuals who have made practical application of the Cayce legacy.

For a free catalog, please write to A.R.E. Press at the address below or call toll free 1-800-723-1112. For any other information, please call 804-428-3588.

> A.R.E. Press
> Sixty-Eighth & Atlantic Avenue
> P.O. Box 656
> Virginia Beach, VA 23451-0656